WHY KOSHER?

WHY KOSHER?
AN ANTHOLOGY *of* ANSWERS

IRVING WELFELD

JASON ARONSON INC.
Northvale, New Jersey
London

For credits, see page 183.

This book was set in 12 pt. Bookman by Alpha Graphics of Pittsfield, N.H.

Copyright © 1996 by Irving Welfeld

10 9 8 7 6 5 4 3 2 1

Library of Congress Cataloging-in-Publication Data

Welfeld, Irving H.
    Why kosher? : an anthology of answers / Irving Welfeld.
        p.   cm.
    Includes bibliographical references and index.
    ISBN 1-56821-606-8
    1. Jews—Dietary laws.   I. Title.
BM710.W29   1996
296.7'3—dc20   96-11441
                                                                CIP

Manufactured in the United States of America. Jason Aronson Inc. offers books and cassettes. For information and catalog write to Jason Aronson Inc., 230 Livingston Street, Northvale, New Jersey 07647.

To My Mother,
For Whom Why Was
A Crooked Letter,

and to

Harriet,
Who Now Reads Labels

"So how about coming back to my place and I'll explain the Jewish dietary laws to you."

Cartoon by Mort Gerberg © 1995. Reprinted by permission.

Contents

Contents xi

Acknowledgments

The author thanks Marilyn Ballotta for her enthusiastic support, Jerry Rosenbaum for going up to Jerusalem in search of an address, and Rabbi Mitchell Wohlberg for introducing me to a rabbi from Barcelona.

1

The Kosher Question—Why?

This is not a cookbook! Of the making of kosher cookbooks, there is almost no end. The only items missing are *The Kosher Tibetan Gourmet*, *Jewish-Eskimo Cuisine*, and *Hints on Cooking for My Child the Astronaut*. I am also not the one to write a cookbook since I have, more than once, been barred from the kitchen of my own home.

The term *kosher* is a Yiddish word derived from the Hebrew word meaning "fit" or "proper." Although generally applied to food, it is also used to describe such nonedible items as Torah scrolls and a shofar (ritual ram's horn). When applied to food, all plants and fruits are kosher. When the food is derived from the animal kingdom, kosher: (1) permits animals that are cud chewers with split hoofs—herbivorous mammals such as cattle, sheep, and goats; (2) permits fish with fins and scales, such as bass and trout; (3) forbids specifically enumerated birds

3

(listed in Leviticus and Deuteronomy) such as eagles and vultures (on the other hand, chickens, ducks, and geese are permitted);[1] and (4) forbids most, but not all, insects. Kosher also requires that animals and birds be ritually slaughtered (*shechita*). The meat must be salted to remove the blood after the carcass has been carefully examined for physical blemishes. The hindquarter is used only if the thigh muscle that is on the socket of the hip has been removed. Meat and milk cannot be cooked or eaten together, and separate utensils must be used.

What is the explanation of these dietary laws? Among the laws of the Torah (see Chapter 2 for the collection of verses dealing with eating), they are considered among the *hukkim* (*hok* in the singular), laws for which there is no obvious explanation. Nevertheless, the Jews accepted the laws even before they heard them, let alone understood them. The first thing was to obey God's instructions, and if there was any time left, then to chew over in their minds what they had bitten off.

Dietary laws were quite common in the ancient world. Different folks had different *hoks*. The Jewish laws are unique to some extent because they are still being observed. More important was how dissimilar the laws of the Jews were from those of their heathen neighbors. The nonpermitted animals were not universally "unclean." They were never demonized. Unkosher food was forbidden only for the Jews and only as food. Jews can play football, even if a pigskin is used. As David Hoffman has written:

Some modern scholars maintain the dietary laws are not exclusive to the Jewish people but were borrowed from other oriental people. . . . [T]he distinction between clean and unclean beasts may be traced to the religion of Zoroaster, which is based on the conflict between Ormuzd the god of light and good, and Ahriman god of darkness and evil. The creation of the former are pure and holy, whilst those of the latter are unclean and abominated.

But this theory is untenable, since the concepts of purity and holiness in Zoroastrian Scriptures and Judaism are not identical. . . . [There are no rival gods in the Bible and the details are different]. For example, all the beasts with uncloven feet such as the horse and the ass and the dog and the fox are according to the Zoroaster clean animals. . . .

. . . [T]he distinction between clean and unclean in the Torah signifies that one class is permitted to be eaten and the others forbidden. Whereas in Zoroastrianism, the unclean beasts constitute the enemies of the deity to be hunted down and destroyed. . . . According to the Torah . . . unclean beasts are merely prohibited as food. [They are not to be hunted down]. On the contrary, we are bidden to show compassion to all animals.[2]

The Torah and the Egyptian dietary laws may both declare that the pig is unclean. The Torah does not give a reason. But better no reason than it is because the pig copulates at a time that is deemed opportune by the demons. As Professor Yehezkel Kaufmann has noted:

Uncleanliness is regarded by heathen cults as a destructive power, bringing evil and sickness. . . . Uncleanliness is bound up with the forces of death in the world of evil spirits that aim at destroying man. . . . The danger is embodied in the actual unclean objects themselves. . . . The Syrians believed that one who eats certain species of forbidden fish is stricken by disease and plague; the Egyptians, that one who drinks the milk of the sow is stricken with leprosy, since the pig is an unclean animal because it copulates when the moon is hidden which is an auspicious time for the demonic world.

. . . [I]n the Bible uncleanliness does not figure as a power at all. . . . Uncleanliness cannot be applied in the Biblical sense to the "unclean" living beast, since a living thing does not defile . . . whereas those fishes, fowl, and grasshoppers forbidden as food are not defiling at all. . . . [N]o destructive power or magical or demonic character resides in them at all.[3]

When the, at present, two largest religious groupings—the Christians and the Muslims—made their appearance, they did not exercise their option to accept the dietary laws. Jesus and his apostles ate kosher. However, for the Christians it was a short fling. The idea that defilement only comes from what goes out of the mouth (Matthew 15:1–20) and the passages in Acts Chapter 10, which include the vision of Peter in which a heavenly voice instructs him to "kill and eat" of all the animals and that baptism cleanses the gentile, made the dietary laws and circumcision expendable. The entire animal kingdom was fair game. The only three prohibitions were food used in idol worship, strangled things, and blood.

The Muslims added swine and carrion; increased the fatal events that disqualified an animal—strangling, beating, falling from a height, being gored or torn to pieces by wild beasts (in contrast to trained falcons) (Koran, Surah 5); and took a new one—intoxicating beverages. They viewed the remaining laws as a richly deserved punishment for those who did not accept Allah's latest teaching.[4]

The Jews have always been a stiff-necked people (which may explain why they are the world's oldest minority and, more important, may explain why they *are*) who did not abide by the views of the majority. They were not all that good in abiding by the views of the One, either. However, in good times and in bad times, they have wanted to understand what they accepted thousands of years ago.

These are the best of times and the worst of times for kosher. Given the disrepute in which Washington and the U.S. Department of Agriculture are held, food products made according to the rules of a Higher Authority are viewed as premium items. The kosher certification is the Good Housekeeping Seal of the 1990s. As of 1993, a total of 23,600 food products bore a kosher symbol. The U.S. sales of all products bearing the kosher seal totaled $35 billion. Kosher companies are attractive takeover targets. Hebrew National is now owned by Conagra (which also owns Armour Bacon); the *balabusta* of Best, Sinai, and Shofar kosher meats and delicatessen is Sara Lee;[5] and Manischewitz is controlled by Kohlberg & Co. and its president came from RJR Nabisco.[6]

It has never been easier to be kosher at home or on the road. The combination of advances in synthetic tastes by the flavor-meisters of the food technology business and the greater use of tofu (the modern Western manna) has produced a kosher eater's Nirvana. The lowly pollock and whiting have been transformed into passable imitations of lobster and crab.

In the area of visual kashruth, there has been much blurring. For millennia, butter was never seen on a table with meat, and cream and coffee never followed the meal. Now, in this golden age of pareve (neither meat nor milk), "chopped liver" is available in dairy restaurants, cheesecake is served for dessert in meat restaurants, and imaginative chefs prepare beef Stroganoff.

The kosher Jewish palate has become multi-ethnic. The diner in New York has the choice of kosher Hunan, Indian, Italian, French, and Moroccan. At the other end of the continent, there are fifty-two kosher restaurants in Los Angeles serving trendy and traditional.[7] In Paris, France, there are sixty kosher eating establishments, a fivefold increase in the last ten years. And Israel's nineteenth McDonald's outlet is kosher. Authentic Big Macs are available but cheeseburgers, milkshakes, and sundaes are not on the menu (in all Israeli outlets the Chicken McNuggets are coated with matzo meal during Passover).[8]

There is less than meets the eye when it comes to Jews eating kosher. Of the 6.5 million people who purposely buy kosher foods, only 1.5 million are observant Jews. The great majority of the shoppers are health-conscious consumers; Seventh Day Adventists; vegetarians looking for meat substitutes or kosher jello and marshmallows that do not contain gelatin (made from ground cow bones or cattle hides),[9] cheese that does not have rennet (made from the intestinal linings of cows), or red lipstick with such names as "Sinai Sienna" or "Promised Land Pink" (one of the most common red pigments, carmine, is derived from the crushed exoskeletons 'of beetle-like cochineal insects);'[10] and less than strictly observant Muslims seeking porkless products.

Kosher meat does not meet the *halal* standard. In order to be *halal*, the slaughtering must be done by a Muslim, the animal must face toward Mecca, and as *each* animal is killed, the prayer "*Bismillah Allah Akbar*" ("In the name of Allah, Allah is great") must be said.[11] Although peace between Jews and Muslims is not at hand in the Middle East, a dual kosher/*halal* product, "My Own Meals," now bears a rabbinic and a *halal* symbol; (kosher and without alcohol) the U.S. Army is requesting bids for multifaith dairy and pareve meals; and Cornell University is offering a course on kosher and *halal* foods.[12]

At present, there are a large number of Jews who eat neither *halal* nor kosher. Most Jews (over 60 percent have no synagogue or Jewish affiliation)[13] belong to the third largest religious group-ing in the world—the nonreligious—for whom ko-sher is a bagel and lox (ethnic blending goes in both directions—"Bagel Bites Fiestas" offers mini-bagels topped with cheese and smoked pork). To the over-whelming majority of Reform and Reconstruc-tionist Jews, contact comes only occasionally—the Passover seder at a grandparent's home or, more likely, the home of a child who has gone "crazy religious" (there's a black hat in almost every fam-ily). For a majority of Conservative Jews, contact is more frequent. They may even have kosher dishes, but these are used only when their parents come for dinner. Among the Orthodox, where kosher is the law, there is a range of compliance—from casual to scrupulous.

We face a paradox. At a time when the avail-ability of kosher products and the opportunities are at an all-time high, the level of observance may be at an all-time low. And, whereas kashrut for cen-turies was chosen in the face of coercion, "treife" (nonkosher) is now freely embraced.

But, then again, why should someone keep ko-sher? As Rav, in a third-century midrash, asked, "For what difference does it make to the Holy One whether one slaughters from the throat or the nape. Or what difference does it make to Him whether one eats unclean or clean subjects."[14] His answer, "The commandments were only given to purify people," is likely to convince only the choir. It is a message that sells no better to a Jew in America in the twen-tieth century than it sold to an enlightened German Jew in the nineteenth century, a cultured Jew in

Moorish Spain in the twelfth century, or a Hellenized Jew in Alexandria in the first century.

Rav's question came from a framework of reverence. The same question often came with a tone of mockery from civilized gentiles. With the coming of the Enlightenment and the walls coming down in Berlin and elsewhere, kosher became a source of embarrassment for the Jew who moved out of the ghetto. It was too oriental for the Jew who wanted to fully partake in the occidental cosmopolitan culture. Living when freedom and reason were more precious than pearls, an enactment to forgo oysters was a painful annoyance. The Reform Movement, struggling with the clash between Judaism and modernity, broke bread in Pittsburgh in November of 1885 and resolved the conflict by casting the dietary laws into the dustbin of history. The laws were discarded in the fourth plank of the Pittsburgh Platform as archaic rituals that obstruct spiritual elevation:

> We hold that all such Mosaic and rabbinical laws regarding diet . . . originated in ages and under the influence of ideas entirely foreign to our present mental and spiritual state. They fail to impress the modern Jew with a spirit of priestly holiness; their observance in our days is apt rather to obstruct than to further modern spiritual elevation.[15]

With a century of experience, it is clear that the removal of the obstruction did not heighten our spiritual elevation. The path of progress is pitted with depressions. Freedom often turns into license,

and the intellect can justify infanticide and genocide. In these post-Aquarian times, *spiritual* to
many modern Jews is more closely associated with
New Age spiritualism, channeling, and crystal gaz-
ing than with Judaism.

The nineteenth-century modernists made reason the litmus test for ritual. However, as Rabbi
Abraham Joshua Heschel noted, "Evaluating faith in
terms of reason is like trying to understand love as
a syllogism and beauty as an algebraic equation."[16]

Jakob Petuchowski, a long-time professor at
the Hebrew Union College (the Reform rabbinical
college), has noted:

> We no longer believe that the European Jew be-
> came a better European and the American Jew a
> better American by shedding his Jewish particu-
> larism. Moreover, in view of what we know today
> about psychology, we have become more circum-
> spect in our evaluation of "ritual" and non-rational.
> If it was the task of Judaism to "adapt" itself to the
> "views and habits of modern civilization," we, today,
> are somewhat more critical of that "modern civili-
> zation." We rather regard it the need of the hour
> to make the nominal Jew into a real Jew. If the
> nineteenth century felt it to be necessary to tell the
> Jew that he no longer had to observe, the twenti-
> eth century faces the task of leading the Jew back
> to the sources of tradition.[17]

Rav's dictum was not the final word in traditional Judaism. Maimonides (or the Rambam—an
acronym for Rabbi Moses ben Maimon) challenged
Rav's dictum. Maimonides believed it was possible

to discern a rational divine purpose in all the commandments. He opposed the generally accepted distinction between *mishpatim*, ordinances that could be explained by human and societal needs, and *hukkim*, statutes for which there was no explanation. To Maimonides, the distinction was that the former had obvious explanation, while the latter had explanations that required great thought and philosophic insight. He had less than kind words towards the believer who found the laws of God incompatible with rational understanding:

> There is a group of human beings who consider it a grievous thing that causes should be given for any law; what would please them most is that the intellect would not find a meaning for the commandments and the prohibitions. What compels them to feel thus is a sickness that they find in their souls. . . . For they think that if these laws . . . had been given to us for this or that reason, it would be as if they derived from the . . . understanding of some intelligent being. If, however, there is a thing for which the intellect could not find any meaning . . . it indubitably derives from God. . . . It is as if, according to these people of weak intellects, man were more perfect than his Maker; for man . . . acts in a manner that leads to some intended end; whereas the deity does not act thus, but commands us to do things that are not useful to us and forbids us to things that are not harmful to us.[18]

Maimonides was challenged almost immediately, both as to specific interpretations and to his notion that the intellect had the key to the mystery of the mitzvoth. The debate has continued over the centuries. Seven hundred fifty years after Maimonides' death, Rav Joseph ber Soleveitchik, the dean of Orthodox American talmudists of his generation, took a position diametrically opposed to Maimonides, arguing that the decision to accept the mitzvoths must be by a metarational process:

> The Bible teaches us that in all of creation man is unique; only he was created in God's image. What is this singular distinguishing characteristic that differentiates man from the animals, plants, and the rest of creation? What endowment reflects the Divine image which is the source of man's status and dignity? Maimonides . . . regarded man's *logos*, his thinking capacity, his ability to acquire knowledge, as man's most singular characteristic. . . .
>
> If man's thinking capacity constitutes his singularity, how could God ask man to commit himself to precepts, the rationality of which eludes him and of which some conflict with his reason? If man's dignity and humanity are rooted in his intellect, would God command a *hukkah*, a *mitzvah*, which is beyond human understanding? . . .
>
> We are, therefore, inclined to follow the masters of the Kabbalah, who taught that not man's rationality but his *ratzon elyon* (higher will) constitutes the singular endowment which distinguishes him from the rest of creation. This will make decisions without consulting the intellect. It is the center of the spiritual personality and constitutes man's real identity.[19]

On the battleground of giants there is much middle ground. For over two millennia, the culinary laws have been examined as carefully as the slaughterer examines the lungs of a chicken. What has been found is a tribute to the mind of man in its analytic and imaginative aspects in delving into a multilayered text. For example, the text states: "You shall not take the mother bird with the young. You shall let the mother bird go" (Deuteronomy 22:6–7). "However, no animal from the herd or from the flock shall be slaughtered on the same day with its young" (Leviticus 22:28).

Most of the commentators agree that God looks after the entire animal kingdom and that man must use his power humanely. However, there the agreement ends. Maimonides focuses on the animal and gives the reason for the laws as respect for the animal's feeling. Nachmanides (Ramban) disagrees, pointing out that if God wanted to pity lower animals, he would not have allowed their killing. His view is that the law is directed at man in order to purge callousness and cruelty. Abarbanel takes an ecological tack. The law is a demonstration that man is not intent on destroying the genus of the animal. Therefore, he retains one to procreate the species. As a variant, Bahya advances the theory that if man would be merciful, as taught by the law of the nest, there never could be genocide.[20]

There is no *one* reason. Rabbi Joseph Leib Bloch suggested that neither are there wrong reasons: "The ultimate truth encompasses all the reasons and all the explanations that have been put forward in the spirit of the Torah."[21] The rest of the book will provide readers with glimpses of the truth.

The second chapter sets out the ground rules—the various verses in the Torah dealing with the dietary rules. The third chapter presents the most oft-given rationale, namely, that the dietary laws promote (usually stated in the past tense as a justification for treating them as outmoded) good health and hygiene. The traditional premise is that God, being the Ultimate Healer, would not give laws that were harmful. It dates back to some of the views of Maimonides and Nachmanides. However, many other commentators rejected this view long before it became a sanctimonious reason for rejecting the laws.

The fourth chapter presents spiritual ("soul food") explanations. The outlooks of the commentators range from seeing the body as the receptacle of the soul to the esoteric kabbalistic traditions in which the eating of kosher food has cosmic significance. A relationship is found, not only to the transmigration of souls, but also to sex and the divine attributes.

The fifth chapter deals with the effect of the dietary laws on Jewish identity and of making and keeping the Jews a holy and separate people. The issue of separation versus assimilation dates back to before Israel was a nation—when Joseph went down to Egypt. It remains relevant in secular, albeit pluralistic, America and in the question of the appropriate Judaic content of the new nation of Israel.

The sixth chapter deals primarily with allegorical and symbolic interpretations of the dietary laws. Two millennia are covered, from Philo of Alexandria, writing in Greek in the first century, to two non-Jews in the twentieth century. The chapter also contains a bit of numerology and subversive political propaganda plus some good words about the pig.

The seventh chapter deals with ecological aspects of the dietary laws. We will get views from the first century, from medieval times, from the nineteenth century, and from a twentieth-century biologist at the University of Wisconsin.

The eighth chapter deals with the ethical features of the laws. Here we will have the famous dispute between Maimonides and Nachmanides on whether the laws were given out of pity to the animals or to teach the humans. In addition, the chapter will describe the ethical implications of a wide range of laws and practices, from slaughtering to keeping separate dishes for meat and dairy.

The ninth chapter deals with the relationship between the laws of kashruth and vegetarianism. It will review the Torah's allusions to the issue and present, among other items, two essays with diametric viewpoints—one that vegetarianism is a step up from kosher and the other that it is a step down.

The tenth chapter will deal with the kosher laws as a pathway to the sanctification of the ordinary. It contains excerpts from works by Leon Kass, a professor at the University of Chicago; Rabbi Abraham Heschel; and the novelist Cynthia Ozick.

NOTES

1. The Torah contains lists of specific fowl that cannot be eaten. From these lists the Talmud derives that permitted birds must possess the following characteristics: (a) they cannot be birds of prey; (b) they should not have a front toe; (c) they must have a craw—their stomach should have a double skin that can be easily separated; (d). they must catch food thrown in the air but lay it on the ground and tear it with their bills before eating. See Seymour Siegel, "A Guide to Observance," in Samuel Dresner, Seymour Siegel, and David Pollack, *The Jewish Dietary Laws* (New York: Rabbinical Assembly of America and the United Synagogue Commission on Jewish Education, 1982), p. 70.

2. Nehama Leibowitz, *Studies in Leviticus* (Jerusalem: World Zionist Organization, 1980), pp. 76–77.

3. "*History of the Israelite Religion,*" in ibid., pp. 77–78.

4. *Encyclopaedia Judaica* 9:93.

5. Edward Silverman, "Kosher Hot Dog Industry Is Losing Family Flavor," *Forward*, September 1, 1995, p. 1.

6. Suein Hwang, "Kosher Food Firms Dive into the Mainstream," *Wall Street Journal*, April 1, 1993, p. B1.

7. Judy Florman, "Kosher Dining in Los Angeles," *Kashrus Magazine—The Magazine for the Kosher Consumer* (Brooklyn, NY), February 1995, p. 26.

8. Haim Shapiro, "Kippot Scarce at Opening of World's First Kosher McDonald's," *Jerusalem Post*, October 12, 1995, p. 2.

9. A kosher certification is insufficient. There is fish gelatin, and some rabbis rule that dry, hard,

marrowless bone (or cowhides) devoid of flesh are permissible. The vegetarian must look for "Japanese" gelatin produced from seaweed. See David Sheinkopf, *Gelatin in Jewish Law* (New York: Bloch Press, 1982).

10. Marcia Mogelonsky,"Kiss Me You Kosher Fool," *American Demographics*, May 1994, pp. 17–18.

11. Albert Fall, "Seeking Ways to Make Food Acceptable to Jews and Moslems," *Cornell Chronicle*, October 1, 1992, p. 3.

12. Joe Regenstein and Carrie Regenstein, "Looking In," *Kashrus Magazine—The Magazine for the Kosher Consumer* (Brooklyn, NY), February 1995, pp. 52–53.

13. Council of Jewish Federations "1990 National Jewish Population Survey," cited in David Rosen, "Survey Links Day School Experience with Jewish Identity," *Yeshiva University Review*, Winter 1995, p. 12.

14. *Midrash Tanhuma*, Parshat Shemini quoted in Robert Alter, "A New Theory of Kashrut," *Commentary*, August 1979, p. 46.

15. Quoted in Bernard Bamberger, "The Dietary Laws," *The Torah—A Modern Commentary* (New York: Union of American Hebrew Congregations, 1983), p. 813.

16. Abraham Joshua Heschel, *Man is Not Alone: Philosophy of Religion* (New York: Noonday Press, 1994), p. 170.

17. Jakob Petuchowski, *Heirs of the Pharisees* (Brown Classics in Judaica, Lanham MD: University Press of America, 1986), pp. 172–173.

18. *The Guide of the Perplexed*, trans. from the Arabic by Shlomo Pines (Chicago: University of Chicago Press, 1963), part 3, 31:523–524.

19. *Reflections of the Rav*, pp. 91–92, quoted in David Hartman, *A Living Covenant* (Glencoe, IL: Free Press, 1985), p. 91.

20. Abraham Chill, *The Mitzvoth—The Commandments and Their Rationale* (Jerusalem: Keter, 1974), pp. 273–274.

21. Elie Munk, *The Call of the Torah—Vayikra*, trans. from the French by E. S. Mazer (Brooklyn, NY: ArtScroll Mesorah Series, 1992), p. 14.

2

Chapters and Verse

MAN THE MASTER IN
A VEGETARIAN PARADISE

"And God created man in His image[,] . . . male and female He created them. God blessed them and God said to them, "'Be fertile and increase, fill the earth and master it; and rule the fish of the sea, the birds of the sky, and all the living and all the living things that creep on earth." God said, "See, I give you every seed-bearing plant that is upon all the earth, and every tree that has seed-bearing fruit; they shall be yours for food. And to all the animals on land, and to all the birds of the sky, and to everything that creeps on the earth, in which there is a breath of life, [I give] all the green plants for food"' (Genesis 1:27–29).[1]

✤

THE NONKOSHER FRUIT

"And the Lord God commanded the man, saying, 'Of every tree of the garden you are free to eat, but as for the tree of knowledge of good and bad, you must not eat of it; for as soon as you eat of it, you shall die' (Genesis 2:16–17).

THE ANIMALS GO CARNIVORE

"When God saw how corrupt the earth was, for all flesh had corrupted its way on earth" (Genesis 6:12).

MAN THE OMNIVORE

"God blessed Noah and his sons, and said to them, 'Be fertile and increase and fill the earth. The fear and the dread of you shall be upon all the beasts of the earth and upon all the birds of the sky—everything with which the earth is astir—and upon all the fish of the sea; they are given into your hand. Every creature that lives shall be yours to eat; as with the green grasses, I give you all these'" (Genesis 9:1–4).

KOSHER LAWS FOR ALL MANKIND

"You must not, however, eat flesh with its life-blood in it" (Genesis 9:5).

❧

THE DANGERS OF DRINK

"Noah, the tiller of soil, was the first to plant a vineyard. He drank of the wine and became drunk, and he uncovered himself within his tent" (Genesis 9:20–21).

❧

WHY JEWS DON'T EAT SIRLOIN

"Jacob was left alone. And a man wrestled with him until the break of dawn. When he saw that he had not prevailed against him, he wrenched Jacob's hip at its socket, so that the socket of his hip was strained as he wrestled with him. . . . The sun rose upon him as he passed Penuel, limping on his hip. That is why the children of Israel to this day do not eat the thigh muscle that is on the socket of the hip, since Jacob's hip socket was

wrenched at the thigh muscle" (Genesis, 30:25–
26, 32–33).

✤

THE PASCHAL LAMB

"Speak to the whole community of Israel and say
that on the tenth of this month each of them shall
take a lamb. . . . You shall keep watch over it until
the fourteenth of the month; and all the aggregate
community of the Israelites shall slaughter it at
twilight. . . . They shall eat that flesh, that same
night; they shall eat it roasted over the fire, with
unleavened bread and with bitter herbs" (Exodus
12:3–7).

✤

TEMPORARY NONKOSHER

"Throughout the seven days unleavened bread
shall be eaten; no leavened bread shall be found
with you, and no leaven shall be found in all your
territory" (Exodus 13:7).

✤

THE SINAI DIET—MANNA
AND OCCASIONAL QUAIL

"In the wilderness, the whole Israelite community grumbled against Moses and Aaron. The Israelites said to them, 'If only we had died by the hand of the Lord in the Land of Egypt, where we sat by the fleshpots, when we ate our fill of bread! For you have brought us into the wilderness to starve this whole congregation to death.'"

"The Lord spoke to Moses: I have heard the grumblings of the Israelites. Speak to them and say: By evening you shall have your fill of bread. . . .

"In the evening quail appeared and covered the camp, in the morning . . . over the surface of the wilderness, lay a fine and flaky substance, as fine as frost on the ground. . . . And, Moses said to them, 'That is the bread which the Lord has given you to eat'" (Exodus 16:2–3, 11–15).

PROHIBITION AGAINST EATING
THE FLESH OF A "TORN" ANIMAL

"You shall not eat any flesh that is torn by beasts in the field, you should cast it to the dogs" (Exodus 22:30).

MILK AND MEAT

"You shall not boil a kid in its mother's milk" (Exodus 23:19, 24:26; Deuteronomy 14:21).

PROHIBITION AGAINST EATING BLOOD

"You shall eat no manner of blood" (Leviticus 7:20).

PROHIBITION AGAINST EATING FAT

"You shall eat no fat of ox or sheep" (Leviticus 7:23).

CUD CHEWERS WITH TRUE HOOFS

"And the Lord spoke to Moses and Aaron, saying to them, speak to the Israelites thus: 'These are the creatures you may eat from all the land animals: any animal that has true hoofs, with clefts through the hoofs, and that chews the cud—such you may eat. The following, however, of those that either chew the cud or have true hoofs, you shall not eat: the camel—although it chews the cud, it has no true hoofs: it is unclean for you; the daman [the Syrian hyrex, any of the several herbivorous mammals of the family Pocaviide, within the order Hyraoida, of Africa and adjacent Asia, resembling woodchuck but more closely related to hoofed mammals] although it chews the cud [only seems to chew], it has no true hoofs: it is unclean for you; the hare—although it chews its cud [only seems to chew], it has no true hoofs: it is unclean for you; and the swine —although it has true hoofs, with the hoofs cleft through, it does not chew its cud: it is unclean for you. You shall not eat of their flesh or touch their carcasses; they are unclean for you" (Leviticus 11:1–8).

✦

SCALES AND FINS

"These may you eat of all that live in water: anything in water, whether in the sea or streams, that has fins or scales—these may you eat. But anything in the sea or in the streams that has no fins or scales, among all the swarming things of the water and among all living creatures that are in the water— they are an abomination for you and an abomination for you they shall remain: you shall not eat of their flesh and you shall abominate their carcasses. Everything in water that has no fins or scales shall be an abomination for you" (Leviticus 11:9–12).

✦

IN THE AIR

"The following you shall abominate among the birds—they shall not be eaten, they are an abomination: the eagle, the vulture and the black vulture, the kite, falcons of every variety, all varieties of raven, the ostrich, the nighthawk, the sea gull; hawks of every variety, the little owl, the cormorant, and the great owl; the white owl, the pelican, and the bustard, the stork, herons of every variety; the hoopee and the bat" (Leviticus 11:13–19).

✦

CHOCOLATE-COVERED
LOCUSTS ARE KOSHER

"All winged swarming things, that walk on fours, shall be an abomination for you. But these you may eat among all the winged swarming that walk on fours; all that have above their feet, jointed legs to leap with on the ground—of those you may eat the following: locusts of every variety, all variety of bald locust; crickets of every variety, and all varieties of grasshopper. But all other winged swarming thing that have four legs shall be an abomination for you" (Leviticus 11:20–23).

✤

YOU SHALL BE HOLY

"For I the Lord am He who brought you up from the land of Egypt to be your God: you shall be holy, for I am holy. These are the instructions concerning animals, birds, all living creatures that move in the water, and all creatures that swarm on earth, for distinguishing between the unclean and the clean, between the living things that may be eaten and the living things that may not be eaten" (Leviticus 11:45–47).

✤

RESPECT FOR ANIMAL LIFE

"Whoever takes in hunting any beast or fowl that may be eaten he shall pour out its blood and cover it with dust" (Leviticus 17:13).

FORBIDDEN FRUITS

"And when you shall come into the land . . . you shall count the fruit as forbidden, three years shall it be forbidden to you, it should not be eaten. And in the fourth year all the fruit of the land shall be holy for giving praise to the Lord" (Leviticus 19:23–24).

PROHIBITION AGAINST
KILLING AN ANIMAL AND
ITS YOUNG ON THE SAME DAY

"However, no animal from the herd or from the flock shall be slaughtered the same day with its young" (Leviticus 22:28).

NOT BY BREAD ALONE

"Man does not live by bread alone, but by the word of God" (Deuteronomy 7:3).

EAT, BE SATISFIED, AND BLESS

"And you shall eat and be satisfied and bless the Lord your God" (Deuteronomy 8:20).

MEAT AS A BLESSING?

"Whenever you desire, you may slaughter and eat meat in any of the settlements according the blessing which the Lord your God has granted you. The unclean and the clean alike may partake of it, as of the gazelle and the deer" (Deuteronomy 12:15).

BLOOD IS PROHIBITED

"But you must not partake of the blood; you shall pour it out on the ground like water" (Deuteronomy 12:16).

✤

EAT MEAT BUT
SLAUGHTER RITUALLY

'When the Lord enlarges your territory as he has promised you and you say, 'I shall eat some meat,' for you have the urge to eat meat, you may eat whenever you wish. . . . [Y]ou may slaughter any of the cattle or sheep that the Lord gives you, as I have instructed you; and you may eat to your heart's content in your settlements. Eat it, however as a gazelle and deer are eaten: the unclean may eat it together with the clean" (Deuteronomy 12:2-22).

PROHIBITION AGAINST EATING
THE LIMB OF A LIVE ANIMAL

"But make sure that you do not partake of the blood; for the blood is the life, and you must not consume the life with the flesh. You must not partake of it; you must pour out it out on the ground like water; you must not partake of it, in order that it may be well with you and with your descendants to come, for you will be doing what is right in the sight of the Lord" (Deuteronomy 12:23–25).

WHAT IS AND WHAT ISN'T
ON THE MENU

"You shall not eat anything abhorrent. These are the animals you may eat: the ox, the sheep and the goat, the deer, the gazelle, the roebuck, the wild goat, the ibex, the antelope, the mountain sheep, and any other animal [the giraffe and the okapi are split hooved cud chewers] that has true hoofs which are cleft in two and brings up the cud—such you may eat. But the following which do bring up the cud or have true hoofs which are cleft through, you may not eat; the camel, the hare and the daman—for although they bring up the cud, they have no true hoofs—they are unclean for you; also the swine—for although it has true hoofs, it does not bring up the cud— is unclean for you. You shall not eat of their flesh or touch their carcasses. These you may eat of all that live in water; you may eat anything that has fins and scales. But you may not eat anything that has no fins and scales: it is unclean for you.

"You may eat any clean bird. The following you may not eat [as listed in "In the Air," with the addition of the buzzard]. . . . All winged swarming things are unclean for you: they may not be eaten. You may eat only clean winged creatures" (Deuteronomy 14:3–20).

SENDING THE
MOTHER BIRD AWAY

"You shall not take the mother bird with the young. You shall let the bird go" (Deuteronomy 22:6, 7).

A LIVING GOD'S PEOPLE DON'T
EAT DEAD ANIMALS

"You shall not eat anything that has died a natural death; give it to the stranger in your community to eat or you may sell it to a foreigner. For you are a people consecrated to the Lord your God" (Deuteronomy 14:21).

✤

DO NOT MUZZLE

"You shall not muzzle an ox when he is treading out the corn" (Deuteronomy 25:4).

✤

NOTE

1. All translations from Harry M. Orlinsly, ed., *The Torah—The Five Books of Moses* (Philadelphia: Jewish Publication Society, 1962).

3

Health Food

HEALTH AND HYGIENE RATIONALE

Doctor God

"We were given a ban by the Torah against all forbidden food. And if there is some among them
whose harm is known [understood] neither by us
nor by the wise men of medicine, do not wonder
about them: The faithful trustworthy Physician
who adjured us about them is wiser than both you
and them. How foolish and hasty would anyone be
who thought nothing is harmful or useful except
as he understands it" (Aaron ha-Levi [Barcelona,
14th century]).[1]

The Dirty Pig

"The purpose of [the dietary laws is] to put an end
to the lusts and licentiousness manifested in what

is most pleasurable and to taking the desire for food and drink as an end."[2]

We shall add to the clarity of this explanation by examining closely the single commandments included therein.

"I say, then, that to eat any of the various kinds of food that the Law has forbidden us is blameworthy. Among all those forbidden to us only pork and fat may be imagined *not* to be harmful. But this is not so, for it is more humid than is proper and contains much superfluous matter. The major reason why the Law abhors is its being very dirty and feeding on dirty things. . . . Now if swine were used as food, market places and even houses would have been dirtier than latrines as may be seen at present in the country of the Franks [Western Europe]. You know the dictum [of the Sages] may their memories be blessed: 'The mouth of the swine is like walking excrement.'

"The fat of the intestines . . . spoils the digestion, and produces cold, thick blood. It is more suitable to burn it. Blood on the one hand and carcasses of beasts that have died, on the other, are also difficult to digest and constitute a harmful nourishment. It is well known that a beast that is terepha [diseased or wounded] is close to being a carcass.

"With reference to the signs marking a permitted animal . . . know that their existence is not in itself a reason for animals being prohibited, they are merely signs by means of which the praised species is discerned from the blamed species" (Maimonides [1134–1204]).[3]

A SUMMARY

   i. The overriding rationale is to curb lust and licentiousness.

  ii. The distinctions of animals based on chewing the cud, split hoofs, and fins and scales have nothing to do with physical well-being.

 iii. The pig is discussed since it does not seem to be harmful. The major reason it is forbidden is that it is a nuisance and a public health menace.

 iv. The items singled out for health reasons— fat, blood, and dead and diseased animals— are at least as appropriate in the twentieth as in the twelfth century. "Thick blood" is another way of saying clogged arteries.

C'mon Pigs of Western Civilization
Eat More Grease

Eat Eat more marbled Sirloin more Pork'n
      gravy!
Lard up the dressing, fry chicken in
      boiling oil
Carry it dribbling to gray climes, snowed with
      salt,
Little lambs covered with mint roast in racks
      surrounded by roast potatoes wet with
      buttersauce,
Buttered veal medallions in creamy saliva,
      buttered beef, by glistening mountains
      of french fries
Stroganoff's in white sour cream, chops
      soaked in olive oil,

surrounded by olives, salty feta cheese, followed
        by Roquefort & Bleu & Silton
        thirsty
for wine, beer Cocacola Fanta Champagne
        Pepsi retsina arak whiskey vodka
Agh! Watch out heart attack, pop more
        angina pills
order a plate of Bratwurst, fried frankfurters,
couple billion Wimpys', MacDonald's burgers
        to the moon & burn!
Salt on those fries! Hot dogs! Milkshakes!
Forget greenbeans, everyday a few carrots,
        a mini big spoonful of salty rice'll
        do, make the plate pretty;
throw in some vinegar pickles, briney sauerkraut
        check yr. cholesterol, swallow a pill
and order a sugar Cream donut, pack 2 under
        the size 44 belt
Pass out in the vomitorium come back cough
        up strands of sandwich still chewing
        pastrami at Katz's delicatessen
Back to central Europe & gobble Kielbasa
        in Łódź
swallow salami in Munich with beer, Liverwurst
        on pumpernickel in Berlin, greasy cheese in
        a 3 star Hotel near Syntagma, on white
        bread thick-buttered
Set an example for developing nations, salt,
        sugar, animal fat, coffee tobacco Schnapps
Drop dead faster! make room for
        Chinese guestworkers with alien soybean
        curds green cabbage & rice!
Africans Latins with rice beans & calabash can
        stay thin & crowd in apartments for working
        class foodfreaks—

Not like western cuisine rich in protein
    cancer heart attack hypertension sweat
    bloated liver & spleen megaly
Diabetes & stroke—monuments to carnivorous
    civilizations
presently murdering Belfast
    Bosnia Cypress Ngomo Karabach Georgia
mailing love letter bombs in
    Vienna or setting houses afire
    in East Germany—have another coffee,
    here's a cigar.
And this is a plate of black forest chocolate cake,
    you deserve it.

Allen Ginsberg[4]

Of Fins and Scales

"The reason why fish and scales [are signs of per-missibility as food] is that those fish that have them always dwell in the upper, clear water, and they are sustained by the air that enters there. Therefore, their bodies contain a certain amount of heat which counteracts the abundance of moistness [of the waters] just as wool, hair, and nails function in man and beast. These fish which have no fins and scales always dwell in the lower turbid water and due to the great abundance of moistness and gathering of water there they cannot repel anything. Hence, they are creatures of cold fluid which cleaves to them and therefore is more easily able to cause death in some waters, such as stagnant lakes" (Nachmanides [Spain, 1097–1194]).[5]

Polluted Bottom Fish

"City health officials have been warning people
since 1987 to eat no more than one meal a week
of local channel catfish, carp, and eel because of
contamination by chlordane and PCBs. Preschool
children, nursing mothers and other women of
childbearing age were urged not to eat any.

"Catfish, carp, and eel are susceptible to the
contaminants because they live on the river bottom and soak up pollution, especially in the
Anacostia River which flows into the Potomac.
Other fish—including bass—are not dangerous."[6]

A Note on Carp

(Nachmanides lived in Spain most of his life and, I
assume, he was unaware of the carp, which has
fins and scales. The carp was indigenous to Asia.
After its introduction into Europe it became the key
ingredient to the most Jewish of all foods, gefilte
fish.)

Forbidden Fruits

"And when you shall come into the land . . . you
shall count the fruit as forbidden, three years shall
it be forbidden to you, it should not be eaten"
(Leviticus 19:23). (This commandment comes only
five verses after the commandment to love thy
neighbor as thyself.) Ibn Ezra (1092–1167) and
Nachmanides both cite health reasons for the fruits
being forbidden.[7]

Holding on to Hygiene

"Isaac M. Wise, the chief organizer of the [Reform] movement in America, publicly advocated the retention of these [dietary] laws for hygienic reasons" (Bernard Bamberger [1904–1980]).[8]

NOT A MATTER OF TASTE

The Pig and Scaleless Fish as Delicacies

"Now of the land animals, the swine is confessed to be the nicest of all meats by those who eat it, and of all aquatic animals the most delicate are the fish which have no scales" (Philo of Alexandria [15-10 B.C.E.–45-50 C.E.]).[9]

I Like Pork, but . . .

"Rabbi Eliezer the son of Azariah said[,] . . . ['A] man should not say . . . I can't abide pork, it is impossible for me to commit incest, but rather, I can, but what shall I do when my Father in Heaven declared such things out of bounds for me?'—from the text: 'I have separated you from the peoples be Mine' He thus separates himself from transgression and accepts upon himself the yoke of Heaven." (Sifra Kedoshim [third century C.E.]).[10]

The Priest and Rabbi Story

The Catholic priest said to the Rabbi: "You don't know what you're missing by not eating bacon. Why would God have created something so delicious if He didn't want people to enjoy it? When are you finally going to break down and try some?" Rabbi: "At your wedding, Father" (Anonymous).

NEITHER HEALTH NOR HYGIENE

Torah Is Not a Minor Medical Treatise

"We would do well to bear in mind that the dietary laws are not as some have asserted motivated by therapeutic considerations. God forbid! Were that so, the Torah would be denigrated to the status of a minor medical treatise and worse than that. . . . [T]he alleged ill effects could be treated by various drugs just as there are antidotes to the most powerful poisons. In that event, the prohibition would no longer apply and the Torah would be superfluous" (Isaac Arami [1420–1494]).[11]

Incomplete as a Health Guide

"If the Torah wished to teach the people how to guard their health, there are many things it should have warned them about. Thus, the Torah prohibited the consumption of camel meat, though it is known that the Arabs eat it and consider it a good and wholesome food" (Samuel David Luzzato [1800–1865]).[12]

"There are creatures well-known for their destructiveness like vipers, adders, and scorpions not mentioned in the list of forbidden by the Torah. There are many likewise poisonous herbs not explicitly forbidden by the Torah. All this merely teaches us that the Divine law did not come to take the place of a medical handbook" (Abarbanel [1437– 1508]).[13]

Man Can Handle the Job of Health

"We may assume that God charged man himself with the mission of discovering the secrets of nature, conquering its deserts, developing the sciences included in the command to Adam to 'fill the earth and subdue it.' Since the Torah offered no guidance on the poisonous properties of certain mushrooms and herbs, but left it to his discretion to find things out for himself, why should it take the trouble of singling out the kind of animals that are the healthiest for man to use for food?" (Nehama Leibowitz [twentieth century]).[14]

Nonkosher Chicken Soup Also Works

"Her [Mimi Sheraton's] next book, just finished, [is] on chicken soup. 'There's only one chapter on Jewish chicken soup,' says Sheraton. 'Whenever you say "chicken soup," everyone thinks Jewish, but in almost every country they give chicken soup to sick people. In China, there are whole ranks of chicken soup according to the illness.'"[15]

Fool Protection

"Know for your own good their reason and their harm [i.e., forbidden foods] were not revealed— for fear that people would rise up who considered themselves very wise, and becoming overwise they would say, 'This harm which the Torah said exists in that thing is so only in that place, since such is its nature; or only for a man whose nature is thus-and-so.' Then some fool may be foolishly persuaded by their words. Because of this their reason was not revealed, to help avoid this stumbling block" (Aaron ha-Levi).[16]

Modern Misconceptions

"Most Jews believe, at least implicitly, that Jewish laws constitute more of a health code than a moral code. They hold the original purpose of Kashruth was to prevent Trichinosis and other maladies. . . .

"Jews who do not observe Kashruth claim it is primarily a health regulation, and because the government now inspects meats, supervises animal slaughter, and utilizes freezers, there are no longer any need to observe Kashruth. . . .

"As for non-Jews, they, like many non-observant Jews, believe Kosher means healthy and clean. They also believe that rabbis bless food to render them Kosher. Millions of Americans believe that somewhere in this country sit groups of rabbis before whom chickens and other animals pass to be blessed" (Dennis Prager).[17]

The Rabbi Is a Scientist

"'The fast-moving pace of science and technology in the area of genetic recombinant research requires that kashrut supervisors be fully conversant with the most recent application of science to food production,' Dr. Tendler said.

"'. . . For example, a gene or two can change a non-kosher to a kosher one by imparting the ability to grow scales. Inserting a bovine gene for rennet into a bacterium that will now manufacture true animal rennet results in a kosher animal rennet even if the original gene is from a non-kosher animal. . . . Talmudic research is needed to determine how many genes can be transferred across special lines without developing a new species'" (Moses Tendler).[18]

PERHAPS A NUTRITION DISCIPLINE

The Food Triangle—Meat, Dairy, and Pareve

"Although kashruth . . . is not observed on the basis of health, the kosher diet creates an excellent format for kosher eating with its categories of meat, dairy, and pareve. We are forbidden to combine the meat/poultry and dairy group (both of which are high not only in protein, but also in cholesterol). But we may eat the pareve whole grains, beans, fruits, and vegetables (which contain the complex carbohydrates and natural nutrients recommended by nutritionists) with either meat or dairy food to provide a balanced diet in every meal. . . . [I]t takes very little effort to provide culinary variety with a kosher diet.

"[W]e are a nutritionist's dream. We are acutely conscious at the point of eating—we stop to recite a blessing before placing anything in our mouths. We wait prescribed periods between meat and dairy. Our very notion of food is linked with limitation and self-discipline. Add to this the value we assign to life and health, and you have the ideal candidate for improved health through dietary modification" (Kenneth Storch).[19]

❧

NOTES

1. *Sefer haHinnuch*, trans. Charles Wengrow (Jerusalem and New York: Feldheim Publisher, 1978), "Sidrah Mishpatim," sec. 73, p. 285.
2. *Guide*, part 3, 35:537.
3. Ibid., part 3, 48:598.
4. *City Lights*, August 1994, p. 22.
5. *Ramban Commentary on the Torah—Leviticus*,

trans. Rabbi Charles Chavel (New York: Shilo, 1974), p. 136.

6. D'vera Cohn, "Local Fish Still Pose Health Risk," *Washington Post*, December 1, 1994, Metro section, p. 3.

7. Chill, *The Mitzvoth*, p. 239.

8. "The Dietary Laws," Gunther Plant, ed., *The Torah—A Modern Commentary* (New York: Union of American Hebrew Congregations, 1983), p. 813.

9. *The Works of Philo*, translated from the Greek by C. D. Yonge (Vinton, VA: Hendrickson, 1993), p. 625. "The Special Laws," part 4.

10. Cited in Leibowitz, *Studies in Leviticus*, p. 84.

11. Ibid.

12. "The Foundations of the Torah," in Noah Rosenbloom, *Luzzato's Ethico-Psychological Interpretation of Judaism* (New York: Yeshiva University, 1965).

13. Cited in Leibowitz, *Studies in Leviticus*, pp. 81–82.

14. Ibid.

15. Felice Maranz, "My Dinner with Mimi," *Jerusalem Report*, December 29, 1994, p. 43.

16. "Sidrah Mishapatim," sec.73, p. 287.

17. "Should a Modern Jew Keep Kosher?" *Brandeis-Bardin Institute Newsletter*, Spring 1988.

18. Moses Tendler, "Symposium of Kosher Law and Modern Technology," *Kashrus Magazine—The Magazine for the Kosher Consumer* (Brooklyn, NY), February 1995, p. 57.

19. Kenneth Storch, "Kosher Living, Healthy Living," in *Body and Soul—A Handbook for Kosher Living* (Brooklyn, NY: Lubavitch Women's Cookbook Publications, 1989), pp. 24–25.

4

Soul Food

KILLER BIRDS; A BLOODTHIRSTY MAN

"The distinguishing mark of a forbidden bird is its carnivorousness. Every bird of prey is invariably unclean for fear that its bloodthirstiness would be communicated to the partaker of its meat through its blood. This may well be the reason of the prohibition of certain animals, since there is no cloven foot cud-chewing animal that preys on others" (Nachmanides).[1]

BAD KARMA

"How can one have a pure clean conscience with the knowledge that his own flesh is the product of a diet of insects, snakes, and other vermin?" (Ibn Ezra [1092–1167]).[2]

OUT OF CHARACTER

"All this comes to teach us that the Divine law did not come to take the place of a medical handbook but to protect our spiritual health. It, therefore, forbade foods which revolt the pure and intellectual soul, clogging the human temperament, demoralizing the character, promoting an unclean spirit, defiling in thought and deed, driving out the pure and holy spirit about which David exclaimed[,] . . . 'The holy spirit take not from me!'; 'A pure heart God created for me,' etc. For this reason the Almighty used the phrase, 'Do not revolt your *souls* with all the vermin . . . ' rather than terming them poisonous or harmful. They were rather unclean and abominating, indicating the spiritual rather than the physical source of their prohibition" (Abarbanel).[3]

THE TONGS OF THE SPIRIT

"At the root of this precept ['and any flesh that is *t'refa* (torn of beasts) in the field you shall not eat'

Exodus 22:30] lies the reason that the body is an instrument of the spirit. Therefore, did it [the spirit] come into its shadow [shelter]. . . . [W]e find the body at its command is like a pair of tongs in the hands of a blacksmith: With it he can produce a tool fit for its purpose.

". . . If the tongs are strong and properly shaped to grasp the tools in them, the craftsman can make them well. If the tongs are not good the tools will never come out properly shaped and fit. In the same way if there is any loss or damage in the body, of any kind, some function of the intelligence will be nullified corresponding to that defect. For that reason our . . . Torah removed us far from anything that causes such defect" (Aaron ha-Levi).[4]

❦

EASES THE PATH TO HOLINESS

"The purpose of the dietary laws . . . is to transform man's body into the proper instrument of his divine spirit, since in Judaism the importance of the body cannot be overestimated. The complex regimen keeps it in a state of purity and holiness as the vehicle of the human soul and the medium of communication of man's spirit with the outer world. . . .

"Great care must be taken, therefore, that this instrument remain sensitive and responsive to serving the spirit. Anything that might negatively affect the human body and deprive it of its fundamental function 'to be an intermediary between the soul of man and the world outside' . . . is forbidden. The observance of the dietary laws does not make a man holy; however, it makes him more receptive to the ennobling influences of the spirit: "One has not achieved holiness simply by observing the dietary laws, but one can then achieve it more easily" (Samson Raphael Hirsch).[5]

WHO KNOWS WHY?

"Who can say whether the saintly character of a particular individual is the result of his diet, education, studies, devotion to Torah or good deeds?" (Nehama Leibowitz).[6]

THE MYSTICAL VIEW

"Maimonides' analysis of the origin of the 'mitzvoth,' the religious commandments, is of great importance, but he would be a bold man who would maintain that his theory of the 'mitzvoth' was likely to increase the enthusiasm of the faithful for their actual practice, likely to augment their immediate appeal to religious feeling. If the prohibition against seething a kid in its mother's milk and many other irrational commandments are explicable as polemics against long forgotten pagan rites . . . —how can one expect the community to remain faithful to practices of which the antecedents have long since disappeared? . . .

"Entirely different was the attitude of the Kabbalists [mystics]. For them the "Halakah" [laws] never became a province of thought. . . . Right from the beginning . . . they sought to master the world of the Halakah as a whole and in every detail. . . . But in their interpretation of the religious commandments these are not represented as allegories of more or less profound ideas, or as pedagogical measures but rather as the performance of a secret rite. . . .

". . . By this transformation of the Halakhah into a sacrament, a mystery rite, by this revival of myth in the very heart of Judaism, the fact remains that it was this transformation which raised the Halakah to a position of incomparable importance for the mystic and strengthened its hold over people. Every mitzvah became an event of cosmic importance, an act which has a bearing on the dynamics of the universe. . . . [I]f the whole universe is an enormous complicated machine, then man is the machinist who keeps the wheels going by applying oil here and there, and at the right time. The moral substance of man's action supplies the "oil" and his existence, therefore, becomes of extreme significance, since it unfolds on a background of cosmic infinitude" (Gershom Scholem [1897–1982]).[7]

GODLY SPARKS

"'Man does not live by bread alone, but by the word of God,' (Deuteronomy 8:3) is a well-known statement from the Torah. The obvious explanation of this verse is that man requires a spiritual dimension in his life and should not simply live to eat, drink and indulge in bodily pleasures. But, it can also be taken quite literally. That it is not the food itself which gives life but the spark of Godliness the 'word of God'—that is in the food.

"The digestive system extracts the nutrients while the *neshama*, the soul, extracts the Godly spark in nature. These 'sparks' are from a higher source in Godliness than even the *neshamas* of man. The Divine energy in every molecule of food is what actually gives us life. Kosher food has a powerful energy that imparts spiritual, intellectual and emotional strength to the Jewish *neshama*. The 'sparks' in nonkosher food, on the other hand, are rooted in an unholy spiritual source. That is why nonkosher food has such an insidious effect" (Tzivia Emmer).[8]

THE ANIMALS FROM THE GOOD SIDE

"The *Zohar* affirms that some animals come from
the side of holiness and some from the side of contamination. A total of ten animals associated with
holiness are listed in Deuteronomy 14:45. They cor-
respond to the ten elements with which God created the universe (*Chagiga* 12a). Rabbi Shimon ben
Yochai quotes the prophet Isaiah (49:3) 'Hashem
[God] takes pride in Israel,' and asks: How could
the Jewish people defile themselves and unite with
the side of contamination? He insists that those
who bear the seal of the king must not stray from
the royal road. That is why the Torah lists those
animals from the good side, for the sake of the
people of Israel" (Elie Munk).[9]

A DIVINE COVENANT WITH THE ANIMALS

"From the beginning of creation, God made a covenant with the animal world. The flesh of certain
animals was to serve as food for man through the
act of ritual slaughter. This gave the animals a
noble purpose—elevation to a higher state of being
through man's consumption" (Yosef Gikatilla [Span-
ish Kabbalist, 1248–1325]).[10]

EATING MEAT UPLIFTS
THE SPHERES OF CREATION

"The whole universe is like a temple where all sing the glory of God (Psalms 29:9). At every rung of the ladder extending from the depths of life on earth to the sublimest regions of the spirit, all the elements reach upward . . . to come ever closer to the holy, divine source of blessings. Indeed, in nature there exists a hierarchial order. . . . This sequential connection of the spheres of creation encompasses the mineral, vegetable, animal, and human realms. The continual rise of each constitutent occurs step-by-step. Thus rain falls on the earth, it waters the earth, it helps the seed to germinate. The seed assimilates and transforms elements of the earth to grow into a plant. The plant is eaten by the animal, and the vegetable element, thanks to this transmigration, reaches a level of existence where the soul begins to shine forth on the purely physical world. Ultimately, man consumes the flesh of the animal, which becomes part of the man himself. The animal comes ever closer to the source of light contained in the spiritual soul. In this way the different elements of nature ascend to the threshold of the metaphysical world, where the unfettered human soul will rejoin the heavenly sphere of absolute holiness" (Moses Cordovero [Safed, 1522–1570]).[11]

THE TRANSMIGRATION OF SOULS

"See now what the pious author of *Sefer Haredim* wrote in chapter 7, page 42a: 'It happened in Castile. A bull was prepared by the Gentiles for their sport (their custom is to beat it and torment it). The night before, a certain Jew had a dream in which his father appeared and said, "Know, my son, that because of my many sins they made me be reincarnated as a bull—the very bull that is prepared to undergo tomorrow the baiting and tormenting that is part of the popular sport. Therefore, my son, redeem me and save me when I escape through such and such a place, lest they kill me and tear me apart. You must pay to redeem me—no matter how much it may cost—and have the bull ritually slaughtered, and let me be eaten by impoverished Torah students. For they have informed me from heaven and permitted me to tell you that in this way you can restore my soul from the level of a beast to the level of a human being, so that I may be worthy of serving God, with His help"'" (Elijah ha-Kohen of Izmir [1674]).[12]

THE COW THAT WENT TO HEAVEN

"Rabbi Meyer Premislaner was exceedingly poor. He made his living by selling the milk from his cow to his neighbors. It was his custom to save some money and distribute it to the poor for the Sabbath.

"Once he had nothing to distribute. Without hesitation, he slaughtered the cow and gave away the meat to the poor. The next morning his wife came crying to him that the cow was missing. Rabbi Meyer answered: 'The cow is not missing; she has gone up to heaven'" (*The Hasidic Anthology*).[13]

WEAKENING THE SEX DRIVE

"The *Zohar* considers that the Jews do not eat the disjointed sinew [see Chapter 2, page 25] because the muscle constitutes the physical support for the genital organs which are the source of the impure elements. [The attacker assumed that sex was the weak point in Jacob's moral armor]. The numerous ramifications of the sciatic nerves surround and fortify these organs. And so, eating this muscle has the effect of attracting the forces of impurity toward man. The muscle bears a name that is derived from the verb to forget; when man eats it, he consequently forgets himself and forgets his obligation to God. Thus, the prohibition is intended to keep the Jewish people from the factor of impurity which is the root of moral and national degradation" (*Zohar*).[14]

BETWEEN THE LINES

Jacob, at the time of the incident, had four wives and twelve children who are mentioned by name—the eleven sons and Dinah.

Genesis rarely reports the arrival of girls. One may assume that there were a significant number of daughters. The men of Shechem were willing to be circumcised in order to marry them (Genesis 34.9).

Rachel was pregnant. The phrase "in the manner of woman" is used in her reply to Laban as the reason she couldn't get off of her camel so that it could be searched for his stolen household idols. There are two ways of being "in the manner of women." One way is pregnancy.

As result of Jacob cursing the thief, Rachel died during childbirth.

After the incident, Jacob did not sire any more children.

FROM FOOD TO SEX TO GOD

"The author (an anonymous 13th century Spanish Kabbalist) raises the question of why human beings are allowed, even commanded to slaughter animals for food. . . . His answer . . . is that eating animals is a way of raising them to a higher level, since they are incorporated into the limbs of their eaters: what they eat becomes us.

The incorporation of food into the body of the eater reaches its end state with the formation of semen. . . . Semen is the most rarefied element of the body. . . . Following the homunculus [little man] theory, semen contains miniature versions of each limb of the body. . . . All lower forms of materiality . . . are transmuted in the seed into a pure substance that has the capacity not only to create new life but also able to influence the very potencies of the divine.

"Digestion is therefore the proper model and analogy for sexuality. Just as the digestive system raises the meat to a higher level . . . physical desire has to be transformed into spiritual intention. But digestion is not just a metaphor, since food is precisely that material substance out of which semen is made. Proper sex, one might say, is the spiritual extension of digestion, as that which started as food becomes semen and finally effects the union of the male and female *sefirot* [Divine emanations]" (*Iggeret haKodesh* [Letter of Holiness]).[15]

NOTES

1. Cited in Chill, *Mitzvoth*, p. 82.
2. Ibid., pp. 178–179.
3. Quoted in Leibowitz, *Studies in Leviticus*, p. 82.
4. "Sidrah Mishpatim," sec. 73, p. 285.
5. Noah Rosenbloom, *Tradition in an Age of Re-*

form—The Religious Philosophy of Samson Raphael Hirsch (Philadelphia: Jewish Publication Society of America, 1976), p. 330.

6. Leibowitz, *Studies in Leviticus*, p. 83.

7. Gershom Scholem, *Major Trends in Jewish Mysticism* (New York: Schocken Paperback, 1961), pp. 29–30.

8. Tzivia Emmer, "The Kashruth Connection— Does God Really Care What I Eat?" Lubavitch Women's Organization, *Body and Soul* (Brooklyn, NY: Lubavitch Women's Cookbook Publications, 1989), p. 7.

9. Munk, *Vayikra*, pp. 101–102.

10. *Sefer Sharei Orah*, in Munk, Vayikra, p. 23.

11. *Pardes Rimmonim*, quoted in Elie Munk, *The Call of the Torah—Genesis*, trans. from the French by E. S. Maser (Jerusalem: Feldheim Publishers, 1980), pp. 203–204.

12. "Restoring the Soul: Eulogy for Jacob Hagiz (1674)," in Marc Saperstein, ed., *Jewish Preaching 1200–1800, An Anthology* (New Haven, CT: Yale University Press, 1989), pp. 305–306.

13. Louis Newman, *The Hasidic Anthology* (New York: Schocken Paperbacks, 1968), p. 12.

14. Munk, *Genesis*, pp. 724–725.

15. David Biale, *Eros and the Jews* (New York: Basic Books, 1992), pp. 105–106.

5

A People Apart

IMPOSED SEPARATION

"They served him by himself [Joseph] and them [his brothers] by themselves, and the Egyptians could not dine with Hebrews, since that would be abhorrent to the Egyptians" (Genesis 43:32).

"If any of the priests or believers eats his meal with a Jew we decide that he does not participate in communion so that he atones" (Council of Elvira [386], Canon 50).[1]

MARCHING TO A DIFFERENT DRUMMER

Meat and Milk

"It is my opinion . . . that idolatry had something to do with it. Perhaps, such food was eaten at one of the ceremonies of their cult or one of their festivals.

A confirmation of this may . . . be found in the fact that the prohibitions against meat [boiled] in milk when it is mentioned the first two times occurs near the commandment concerning pilgrimage: 'Three times a year and so on.' It is as if it had said: When you go on pilgrimage and enter the house of the lord your God, do not cook there in the way they used to do" (Maimonides).[2]

"Ancient inscriptions unearthed by archaeologists . . . tend to confirm that this was a fertility rite. J. G. Frazer, quoting a Karaite medieval author, writes: 'There was a custom among the ancient heathens, who when they had gathered all the crop, used to boil the kid in the mother's milk.'"[3]

Don't Eat Little Green Apples under Ashera's Tree

"In order to keep people away from all magical practices, it has been prohibited to observe any of their usages, even those attaching to agriculture and pastoral activities. . . . This is the meaning of the dictum: *And ye shall not walk in the customs (hukkot) of the nation* [Leviticus 20:23] . . .

The idolaters have . . . one tree, namely, the *ashera* . . . consecrated to the object of their worship. . . . They have also prescribed that [of] the first fruit of every tree whose fruits are edible . . . a portion of them should serve as an offering while the rest should be eaten in an *idolatrous temple*. They have also spread abroad the opinion that . . . [if not done] the tree would wither. . . . Inasmuch as men were afraid for their property, they likewise hastened to perform the practices. Accordingly the law opposed this opinion and He [God] . . . commanded that everything produced in the course of three years by a tree whose fruits are edible should be burnt" (Maimonides).[4]

The worship of the goddess Asherah was particularly prevalent. In 622 B.C.E., only a few decades before the Babylonian exile, the Judean king Josiah carried out a sweeping reform in which he destroyed the house in the Temple where the "women wove clothes for Asherah" (2 Kings 23:7). Asherah figurines were also found in the Sinai, dating from the same period, with blessings to "YHWH and to his Asherah" implying that the Hebrew God had a Canaanite consort.[5]

A Little Bit of Etymology

"Although the word 'hukkoth' is derived from the root 'hakak' (to legislate), it was also brought into relation with the verb 'hakah' which means to imitate. Any imitation of non-Jewish ways could thus be brought under the biblical prohibition of the 'statutes of the Gentiles' ['You shall not do as they do in the land of Egypt . . . and you shall not do as they do in the land of Canaan. You shall not walk in their statutes' Leviticus 18:3]" (Jakob Petuchowski).[6]

Dance in a Different Dance Hall

The prohibition of using wine produced or handled by non-Jews was originally enacted to prevent participation in Dionysian pagan rites. It was rab-

binically extended even to the God-believing
Gentile world to avoid revelry that could lead to
intermarriage.

✦

SEPARATION AS AN ATTRACTION
TO MYSTERY SEEKERS

"From Hellenistic Jewish circles we have the so-
called *Letter of Aristeas*, dated variously between
200 B.C.E. and post 33 C.E. . . . . The book is particularly emphatic on the point of Jewish separatism.
It glories in the dietary laws by which 'we have been
distinctly separated from the rest of mankind' and
it is grateful to the lawgiver (Moses) who 'fenced us
around with impregnable ramparts and walls of
iron that we may not mingle at all with any of the
other nations.' Yet withal, modern scholars have
no trouble detecting in this tract, one of the many
propaganda attempts to convert Greek-speaking
Gentiles to Judaism. . . .

"Far from soft-pedaling Jewish separation and
particularism, the Hellenistic Jewish writers em-
phasized them . . . even though the very existence
of such propaganda literature was evidence enough
of the universalistic Jewish 'out-reach.' They must
have been guided by experience in what they were
doing. Perhaps they even took a leaf out of the book
of the Hellenistic mystery cults, which, in spite of
all the 'mystery' must have been constantly on the

lookout for new initiates, and which possibly just *because* of their mystery-making and secretiveness were never lacking in new applicants" (Jakob Petuchowski).[7]

✦

SEPARATION AND HOLINESS

The Written Word

"For I the Lord am He who brought you up from the land of Egypt to be your God; you shall be holy for I am holy. These are the instructions concerning animals, birds, all living creatures that move in the water, and all the creatures that swarm on earth, for distinguishing between the unclean and the clean, between the living things that may be eaten and the living things that may not be eaten" (Leviticus 11:45–47).

Holy and Separate: From the Same Word

"Kashruth is one of the firmest ramparts of the particularistic aspect of Judaism. It demands sacrifice, self-discipline, and determination—but what that is really worthwhile in life does not? It demands the courage to turn our face against the powerful current of conformity that almost overcomes us daily, not only against the gentile world . . . but against the majority of the *Jewish* world thus standing as a witness to God amongst our own nation as well as the 'nations.'

". . . The goal of Kashruth is holiness, a holy man, and a holy nation. It is part of Judaism's attempt to hallow the common act of eating, which is an aspect of our animal nature. It likewise sets us apart from the nations. Thus it achieves its objective, holiness, in two ways, both of which are implied in the Hebrew word 'Kadosh': inner hallowing and outer separateness. Finally, Kashruth makes two demands upon the modern Jew: understanding of the mind and commitment of the will. Both are indispensable" (Samuel Dresner).[8]

A Holy People

God brought Israel out of Egypt to be a "holy people"[:] . . . a people apart distinguished from all others by outward rites. . . . Outward consecration was symbolically to express an inner sanctity. This thought of being a 'holy people' . . . [means being] a witness to God's sovereignty and purity. He made a kingdom of priests sanctified in themselves for the rest of the world's sake—this sublime thought would daily be impressed on the mind and these Commandments which separated from other nations. This would, furthermore, prevent a close and intimate association with heathens which would result in complete absorption" (J. H. Hertz [1872–1947]).[9]

JEWISH IDENTITY

Catholic Outside/Jewish Inside

Among those who stayed behind [in Spain] were Jews who pretended to convert to Roman Catholicism, but who maintained a practice of Judaism. The term 'Marrano' was at one time used to describe them, as the term refers to the swine which they publicly eat to demonstrate their outward conversion. . . .

"In Majorca, the community was converted in the 1430's and are called Chuetas, from "pork lard" since they regularly keep pork lard boiling in cauldrons on their porches. They themselves still call themselves Israelitas in private and ask forgiveness from el Grande Dio for worshipping in front of statues of a man. They typically sacrificed (in a figurative . . . sense) their first born sons to the Catholic priesthood as a means of getting protection from Church persecution, so, ironically, many of the priests across the Baleiric Islands are from Marrano families."[10]

A Racial Allegiance

"The dietary laws have proved an important factor in the preservation of the Jewish race in the past, and are, in more than one respect, an irreplaceable agency for maintaining Jewish identity in the present. An illustrious Jewish scientist wrote:[11] 'It might appear to be a minute matter to pronounce the Hebrew blessing over bread, and to accustom one's children to do so. Yet if a Jew at the partaking of food, remembers the identical blessing used by his fellow Jews from time immemorial and the world over, he revives in himself, wherever he be at the moment, communion with his imperishable race. . . . [T]he Jew who keeps Kashruth has to think of his religion as a communal allegiance on the occasion of every meal; the observance of those laws constitute a renewal of acquiescence in the fact he is a Jew and a deliberate acknowledgement of the fact.'"[12]

The Jewish Home

"For the Jewish woman, the kitchen is the field in which she sows the seeds of national survival, in which she implants Jewishness in her family. Here in the preparation and serving of kosher food she can do more to instill Jewish values to her children than a hundred trips to a Judaica museum or even hours spent in a synagogue. With her pots and pans, the Jewish woman warms souls and vanquishes cynicism and indifference. While she may execute her responsibilities on many fronts—in her community, at the workplace, in the schools—it is her kitchen that she exerts the most profound influence. She nurtures the future Jewish nation by following the dietary laws given in the Torah. . . .

"There are no double messages or mixed signals here: a woman feeding her children a diet of kosher food is making a clear statement for their Jewish identity. Without Kashrut, a family is essentially bereft of Jewishness" (Tziporah Muchnik).[13]

The Jewish in the Jewish Community Center

"In the name of Jewish loyalty, leading Reform rabbis have urged that the right of all Jews to live by the dietary laws (if they so choose) should be protected. Therefore, Reform Jews should insist that Jewish communal institutions provide kosher food for those who desire it. Reform rabbis should also know something about the meaning of the laws" (Bernard Bamberger [1904–1980]).[14]

Jewish with the Folk; One of the Guys with the Gentiles

"Once these practices lose their character as laws and become folkways, Jews will be able to exercise better judgement as to the manner of their observance. Moreover, since the main purpose of these practices is to add Jewish atmosphere to the home, there is no reason for suffering the inconvenience and self-deprivation which results in a rigid adherence outside the home. From the standpoint urged here it would not be amiss for a Jew to eat freely in the house of a Gentile and to refuse from eating *trefa* in the home of a fellow Jew. By this means, dietary practices would no longer foster the aloofness of the Jew, which, however, justified in the past, is totally unwarranted in our day" (Mordecai Kaplan).[15]

Double Standards Lead to No Standards

"Once I was taken on a journey by my parents and at the hotel where we dined the fat and the lean were mixed, and cheese was served after meat. Even ham appeared on the table. My parents ate and permitted me to eat of this forbidden dish. Then the food forbidden at home was no longer forbidden when one was away from home? The law was law no longer" (Edmund Fleg).[16]

Orphans among the Nations

"Philo felt that the difference between the Jews and non-Jews are unlike the differences that may exist between religious groups of non-Jews. The former are more fundamental. They place the Jews as a group apart from the totality of non-Jews, with all the varieties of religions and sects among the non-Jews themselves. Whenever any hostility breaks out between two groups of non-Jews, he says, the hostile groups do not stand alone, for 'by reason of their frequent intercourse with other nations they are in no want of helpers who join sides with them.' Not so, however, is the case of the Jews. 'The Jewish nation has none to take its part' and 'one may say that the whole Jewish nation is in a position of an orphan compared with all other nations in other lands'" (Harry Austryn Wolfson).[17]

Only in America—Fighter Jets and Kosher Lunches

"The 1972 Florida primary drew eleven Democratic presidential candidates, including Sens. Hubert Humphrey of Minnesota and Henry M. 'Scoop' Jackson of Washington. No constituency was more assiduously courted than the Jews who had fled New York, Philadelphia, and Chicago for South Florida.

"Trumpeting his devotion to the defense of Israel, Scoop Jackson all but pledged to personally escort U.S. figher jets to Tel Aviv on his inauguration day. But he was outdone by Hubert Humphrey. In a Miami speech, the Minnesotan expressed his shock at the discovery that the United States failed to provide a kosher menu as part of the nation's public school lunch program" (Mark Shields).[18]

If You're with the Folks, Everything Goes

"I don't have to be religiously Jewish to distinguish myself from the Gentiles. When I'm here [Israel] I don't have to think, Is the woman I meet Jewish? I don't care if she is Jewish, because if I met her here, and she's able to speak Hebrew[,] . . . she's Jewish enough for me. I don't have to worry about eating Jewish food to demonstrate culinary solidarity. I don't need a delicatessen to show that I'm Jewish" (Ze'ev Chafetz).[19]

"(Mr. Chafetz took a Gentile spouse in 1994. It's unclear whether she speaks Hebrew)."[20]

The Ultimate Jewish Parochials

"How, by the way, do we recognize the parochial? . . . It is the point of view that dismisses as parochial a civilization not one's own. And it is, sometimes, the point of view that characterizes Jews, who, for whatever reason, personal or political, are not much interested in Jewish ideas. Such persons

(unlike most Gentiles who have severed any serious connection with Christianity) call themselves
'universalists.' It is striking to observe that univer-
salism of this sort is, however, the ultimate Jewish parochialism. It is mainly Jews who profess it"
(Cynthia Ozick [1928–]).[21]

IT'S THE HOLINESS THAT COUNTS, NOT THE SEPARATION

Religious Survival, Not National Survival

"[Yeshayahu] Leibowitz refuses to allow Judaism
to become an instrument for securing group survival. He is fiercely critical of applying religious
models such as . . . sanctification of God's name,
to the heroism of Israel soldiers in battle. For
Leibowitz, to so do is idolatrous, since it substitutes
for loyalty to God. Patriotism must never be con-
fused with the life of worship. . . . The intimate
connection with Jewish nationhood must never
lead to the approach of Mordecai Kaplan, who understood Judaism as a civilization that promotes
and secures the survival of the Jewish people. All
attempts to explain Judaism as providing for the
meaningful continuity of the Jewish people in history are considered by Leibowitz as modern forms
of idolatry. 'Mitzvah' is not an instrument for Jewish continuity. . . . [N]ationhood has significance

only because 'mitzvoth' and worship of God have eternal meanings"[22]

Reading the Text Differently

"Some tend to regard these laws as designed to make a fundamental cleavage between the Jewish people and other nations. . . . A special diet was imposed on the Jewish people to make them feel separate or specially singled out as a holy nation, as the people of the Lord.

"We cite the following verses ["The Written Word," page 75]. . . . The foregoing passage is liable to present a misleading picture of the true reason for these laws, giving the impression that they were designed to serve merely as an external sign of distinction for the Jewish people as a kingdom of priests. But, in actual fact, the verses quoted make no mention of the idea that certain foods were prohibited in order to separate them from the nations. On the contrary, it is stated since God has separated the Jewish people from other peoples, Israel is obliged to observe the Divine precepts that teach us to make a difference between clean and unclean beasts, just the same as Israel is obliged to keep other precepts" (David Hoffman).[23]

A Separation for Self-Discipline

"Every Jew must be set apart in laws and way of life from the nations and not imitate their deeds, always cleaving to God. . . . But besides this reason which varies in time and place (for instance, if all

the world were to worship the true God and keep
just laws, this separation would not be necessary),
the multiplicity of precepts is of benefit at all times
and places in improving our moral behavior on two
counts: (1) the precepts we observe make us remember at every moment of the God who commanded them. . . . [This] implants in us the fear of
God that we should not sin. (2) The only method
by which man can overcome his passions and rule
over himself lies in habituating himself to foregoing material enjoyments and the endurance of
pain and straitened circumstances. . . . The philoso-
pher Epictetus states that if one placed the following two words on his heart, he would be certain not
to sin and these are they—'Sustine et abstine,' i.e.
'endure and abstain' from pleasures. The numerous *mitzvot* and statutes accustom man to exercise
self-control" (Samuel David Luzzato).[24]

The Intimate and the Ethical

"Though the Jewish people and Judaism share and
reflect universal needs . . . there are also features
in Jewish spirituality that symbolically reflect the
particular history and existence of the Jewish people.
. . . Many of those *hukkim* are mitzvoth that struc-
ture Jewish particularity and provide a vivid framework for expressing the community's particular passion for its God, resemble intimate family customs.
. . . They complement and absorb the ethical. They
enhance the richness of Jewish religious consciousness by widening one's appreciation of the complex-
ity of the nonrational dimension in Judaism. . . .

"Ethical seriousness is not the only value in the covenantal appreciation of the religious life; the community and social action do not exhaust the yearning of the religious soul for God. Prayer, religious awe and the nonrational retain their place in the religious life. . . .

"A single-minded vision . . . undermines the richness that Judaism allows one to appreciate in its integration of the passion of covenantal particularity with concern for the social and political well-being of humankind. Nor . . . should the covenantal intimacy with God expressed through the *hukkim* lead one to build a covenantal identity that focuses on Jewish separateness and distinctiveness from the world. . . . Judaism, as a total way of life, can never be defined only by what sets it apart from the rest of the world" (David Hartman).[25]

❧

AN ADVANCE PARTY FOR THE NATIONS

A Treasure for Humanity

"What is the special function of our people, and of the Jew as an individual? . . . By a simple process of elimination, we can . . . determine the essential character and function of our people.

". . . [A] survey of our long history . . . will at once bring to light [that] . . . it was not material wealth, nor physical strength[;] . . . it was not statehood or homeland [as] . . . most of the time . . . our people possessed no independent state[;] . . . it was not the language [as] . . . even in Biblical times Aramaic began to supplant the Holy Tongue as the spoken language[;] . . . [n]or was it any common secular culture that preserved our people, since that changes radically from era to era.

"The one and only common factor which has been present with Jews throughout the ages, in all lands, and under all circumstances, is the Torah and mitzvot, which Jews have observed tenaciously in their daily lives. . . . Hence the logical conclusion: the policy of imitating the other nations, far from helping preserve the Jewish people, rather endangers its very existence. . . .

"The secret of our existence is our being 'a people that dwells alone' (Numbers 23:9) . . . believing in one God, leading a life according to one Torah which is eternal and unchangeable. Our 'otherness' and independence of thought and conduct are not our weakness but our strength. Only in this way can we fulfill our function imposed on us by our Creator, to be unto God a 'kingdom of priests and a holy nation' thereby also being a 'segula' (treasure) for all of humanity" (Lubavitcher Rebbe).[26]

An Advance Party

"Forbidding cruelty to animals, prohibiting the consumption of blood—these are the bases for most of the . . . [Jewish laws] of slaughtering animals (*shehita*) and of preparing meat for food. . . . But

. . . they are addressed to the sons of Noah, that is to all humanity, which brings out the universal value of the biblical principles. Indeed, there can be but one truth, valid for Jew and non-Jew alike. The difference is that for the Jews, who are the 'advance party' of the nations, the duties are more numerous and stricter than for the others" (Elie Munk).[27]

Parochial and Catholic

"It is our duty to praise the Master of all, to ascribe to the Molder of primeval creation, for He has not made us like the nations of the lands, and has not emplaced us like the families of the earth; for He has not assigned our portion like theirs, nor our lot like all their multitude. . . .

"Therefore we put our hope in you Hashem our God that we may soon see Your mighty splendor . . . to perfect the universe through the Almighty's sovereignty. Then all humanity will call upon Your Name, to turn all the earth's wicked toward You. All the world's inhabitants will recognize and know that to You every knee should bend, . . . and they will all accept upon themselves the yoke of Your kingdom, that You may reign over them soon and eternally. For the kingdom is Yours and You will reign for all eternity in glory, as it is written in thy Torah: 'Hashem shall reign for all eternity.' And it is said: 'Hashem will be King over all the world— on that day Hashem will be One, and His Name will be One'" (Alenu).[28]

NOTES

1. Quoted in Jane S. Gerber, *The Jews of Spain* (New York: Free Press, 1994), p. 6.

2. *Guide*, part 3, 48:599.

3. *Encyclopaedia Judaica* 6:44.

4. *Guide* 3, 37:543, 546–547.

5. Biale, *Eros and the Jews,* p. 27.

6. Petuchowski, *Heirs of the Pharisees*, p. 45.

7. Ibid., pp. 12–13.

8. Dresner, "Their Meaning For Our Time," in *The Jewish Dietary Laws*, pp. 53–54.

9. Rabbi J. H. Hertz, ed., *The Pentateuch and the Haftorahs* (Metzudah, 1937), 1:448.

10. "Frequently Asked Questions on Soc.Culture. Jewish," *PSI NET*, Last Post: Jan. 3, 1995, Part 7: Jews as a Nation, Subject 13.5.

11. W. M. Haffkine, "A Plea for Orthodoxy," *Menorah Journal*, April 18, 1916, 2:71, 76.

12. Hertz, *Pentateuch* 1:448.

13. Tziporah Muchnik, "Am I Feeding an Army . . . or Nurturing a Nation?" Lubavitch Women's Organization, *Body and Soul* (Brooklyn, NY: Lubavitch Women's Cookbook Publications, 1989), pp. 9–10.

14. Bamberger, "The Dietary Laws," in *The Torah— A Modern Commentary* p. 813.

15. Mordecai Kaplan, *Judaism as a Civilization* (New York: Schocken Books, 1967), pp. 441–442.

16. *Why I am a Jew*, quoted in Dresner, "Their Meaning For Our Time," p. 45.

17. Quoted in Leo Schwartz, *Wolfson of Harvard— Portrait of a Scholar* (Philadelphia: Jewish Publication Society of America, 1978), p. 152.

18. Mark Shields, "Return of the Pander Bear," *Washington Post*, January 19, 1995, p. A25.

19. Thomas Friedman, *From Beirut to Jerusalem* (New York: Farrar, Strauss, Giroux, 1989), pp. 294–295.

20. Ze'ev Chafetz, "A Wedding in Exile," *Jerusalem Report*, October, 24, 1994, p. 26.

21 Cynthia Ozick, "Towards New Yiddish," in *Art & Ardor* (New York: Alfred A. Knopf Inc., 1983), p. 153.

22. David Hartman, *A Living Covenant* (Glencoe, IL: Free Press, 1985), pp. 114–115.

23. Quoted in Leibowitz, *Studies in Leviticus*, p. 83.

24. Ibid., p. 85.

25. Hartman, *A Living Covenant*, pp. 96–97.

26. "The Common Denominator," *L'Chayim Newsletter for All Jews*, September 12, 1992.

27. Munk, *Genesis*, p. 205.

28. Concluding prayer of the morning, afternoon, and evening services. See Nosson Scherman and Meir Zlotowitz, eds., *The ArtScroll Weekday Siddur*, trans. Nosson Scherman (Brooklyn, NY: Mesorah, 1988), pp. 159, 161.

6

Numerology, Allegories, and Symbols

A LITTLE NUMEROLOGY

"The animals which are clean and lawful to be used as food are ten in number; the heifer, the lamb, the goat, the stag, the antelope, the buffalo, the roebuck, the pygarga [an antelope with a white rump], the wild ox and the chamois, for he [Moses] always adheres to arithmetical subtilty which, as he originally devised it with the minutest accuracy possible, he extends to all existing things. . . .

"Now of all the numbers beginning from the unit, the most perfect is the number ten, and as Moses says, it is the most sacred of all and a holy number, and by it he now limits the races of animals that are clean, wishing to assign the use of them to all of those who partake in the constitution which he is establishing" (Philo of Alexandria).[1]

❧

A LOT OF ALLEGORY

"And he [Moses] gives two tests[:] . . . first they must part the hoof, secondly they must chew the cud; for those that do neither or only one of these things, are unclean" (106).

"For all the animals which chew the cud[,] . . . in the same manner, the man who is being instructed, having received the documents and speculations of wisdom in at his ears from his instructor, . . . but still is not able to hold it firmly and to embrace it all at once, until he has resolved in his mouth everything which he has heard by the continued exercise of the memory, . . . and then impresses the image of it all firmly on his soul" (107).

". . . [T]he firm conception of these ideas is of no advantage to him unless he is able to discriminate and distinguish which . . . to choose and which to avoid, . . . the parting of the hoof is the symbol; since the course of life is twofold, the one leading to wickedness and the other to virtue. . . . We must renounce the one and never forsake the other" (108).

What Beasts Are Not Clean

"For this reason all animals with solid hoofs, and all with many toes are . . . unclean; the one because . . . they imply that the nature of good and evil are one and the same; which is just as if one were to say that the . . . road up hill and down hill were the same. And the other, because it shows that there are many roads, though . . . they have no right to be called roads at all . . . for it is not easy among the variety of paths to choose that which is most desirable and the most excellent" (109).

What Aquatic Animals Are Clean

". . . [H]e proceeds to describe which aquatic creatures are clean and lawful to be used as food; distinguishing them also by two characteristics as having fins or scales . . . and those having only one of the two, he rejects and prohibits" (110).

". . . [A]ll those creatures which are destitute of both, or even of one of the two, are sucked down by the current, not being able to resist the force of the stream; but those which have both these characteristics can stem the water, and oppose it in the front and strive against it as against an adversary, and struggle with invincible good will and courage, so that if they are pushed they push back in their turn; and if they are pursued they turn on their foe and pursue it in their turn, making themselves broad roads in a pathless district, so as to have an easy passage to and fro" (111).

"Now both of these things are symbols; the former of a soul devoted to pleasure, and the latter of one who loves perseverance and temperance. For the road that leads to pleasure is a downhill one and very easy. . . . But the path which leads to temperance is up hill and laborious, but advantageous. One leads men downwards, and prevents those who travel it from retracing their steps until they have arrived at the very lowest bottom, but the other leads to heaven; making those who do not weary before they reach it immortal" (112).

About Reptiles

". . . [T]hose reptiles which have no feet, and which crawl onwards, dragging themselves along the ground on their bellies, or those which have four legs, or many feet are all unclean as regards their being eaten.

"And here again, . . . he intimates under a figurative form of expression those who are devoted to their bellies, gorging themselves like cormorants, and who are continuously offering up tribute to their miserable belly, tribute, that is, of strong wine, and confections, and fish, and in short, all the superfluous delicacies which the skill and labor of bakers and confectioners, are able to devise, inventing all sorts of rare viands, to stimulate and set on fire the unsatiable and unappeasable appetites of man.

"And when he speaks of animals with four legs and many feet, he intends to designate the miserable slaves of not one single passion, appetite, but of all the passions; the genera of which there are four in number; but in their subordinate species they are innumerable. Therefore, the despotism of one is very grievous, but that of many is most terrible" (113).

". . . [I]n the case of those reptiles who have legs above their feet, so that they are able to take leaps from the ground, those Moses speaks of as clean;

as, for example, the different kind of locusts, and that animal called the serpent-fighter, here again intimating by figurative expression the manner and habits of the rational soul. For the weight of the body being naturally heavy, drags down with it those who are but of small wisdom, strangling it and pressing it down by the weight of the flesh" (114).

Concerning Flying Creatures

". . . [T]he remaining class of animals in the air, the innumerable kinds of flying creatures, [he rejects] all of those that prey on one another or on man, all carnivorous birds, in short, all animals which are venomous, and all which have any power of plotting against others" (116).

"But doves and pigeons, and turtle-doves, and all the flocks of cranes, and geese, and birds of that kind he numbers in the class of domestic, and tame, and eatable creatures, allowing everyone to partake of them with impunity" (117).

"Thus, in each of the parts of the universe, earth, water, and air, he refuses some kinds of each description of animal, whether terrestrial, or aquatic, or aerial, to our use; and thus, taking as it were fuel from the fire, he causes the extinction of appetites" (118).

Philo of Alexandria[2]

MAIMONIDES NOT IMPRESSED

"In my opinion, all those who occupy themselves with finding causes for something of these particulars are stricken with a prolonged madness in the course of which they do not put an end to incongruity, but rather increase the number of incongruities. Those who imagine that a cause may be found for suchlike things are far from the truth" (Maimonides).[3]

SYMBOLIC LANGUAGE OF THE HOLY

"The traditional symbolic approach . . . err[s] on the side of excessive specificity of explanation. The impulse here, beginning with Philo of Alexandria, who tried to rationalize Scripture through the supple Greek instrument of allegory, is to sublimate the . . . particularities of the dietary prohibitions . . . by assigning to them specific spiritual significance, in an elaborate language that the stomach, as it were, is made to speak to the soul. . . . [A]ny symbolic interpretation . . . entails enormous homiletic strain, but, oddly enough, a newfangled version of the symbolic approach has produced the most plausible view of how the dietary laws function as a central institution of biblical religion.

"The symbolic approach was first redefined . . . by the British anthropologist Mary Douglas in her lucid study *Purity and Danger* (1966). Now it has

been extended in a challenging way by Jean Soler
. . . in "The Dietary Prohibitions of the Hebrews"
recently published in the *New York Review of Books*
(June 14, 1979). . . .

"The underlying [shared] perception . . . is that
the dietary prohibitions are a kind of language,
which is able, through a syntax of actions, rather
than words, to order the world along the lines of a
particular sense of reality. . . . The catalogue of
forbidden foods in Leviticus 11 is explicitly linked
in the text with the idea of Israel being holy, even
as God is holy, and so Mrs. Douglas quite sensi-
bly construes the dietary rules as a symbolic system intended to express the concept of holiness
which . . . she defines as 'unity, integrity, perfection of the individual and the kind.'

". . . Douglas concludes that 'In general the underlying principle of cleanness in animals is that
they shall conform wholly to their class. Those
species are unclean which are imperfect members
of their class, or whose class confounds the general scheme of the world.' Thus, the pig does not
conform to the perfect model of the domesticated
meat animal in a pastoral culture because it is not
a ruminant, though it has cloven hoofs. Amphibians and reptiles are the prime model of the unclean creatures in this gastronomic language of the
holy because they belong to more than one element
and because they exhibit an improper means of
locomotion for their elements, neither swimming
nor walking but slithering and 'swarming.'

"[Soler] develops at length a notion very similar to her central idea of taxonomic consistency,

putting particular emphasis on the horror of the hybrid for the Hebrew imagination, whether it is an animal that seems to straddle two realms, a human transvestite, or even a fabric woven of linen and wool. . . .

"In precisely this regard, the diametric contrast with the Greeks—a consideration not part of Soler's argument—is instructive. Greek literature from Hesiod revels in monstrosity, savors the piquant hybrid character of man-god, man-beast, androgynous, and metamorphic figures, biblical literature preferring realms to be distinct and generic identities. . . . Soler, in a similar vein, shrewdly observes the decisive break between Judaism and Christianity came when the founders of Christianity chose to see Jesus as a God-man, for such a hybrid violated a basic assumption of the Hebrew imagination that had been expressed for over a millennium in everything from theology . . . to social institutions and dietary laws.

"Soler develops another suggestive implication of the principle of taxonomic consistency in arguing that biblical legislation strove to keep separate not only entities generically opposed but also those that exhibited a dangerous closeness. In this fashion, he can bracket together the biblical incest taboo with the enigmatic ban on cooking a kid in its mother's milk, wittily observing: 'You shall not put a mother and her son in the same pot, any more than into the same bed.' For this would violate the basic ordering principle[,] . . . 'everything belongs to one species only, one people, one sex, one category[—] . . . one God.'

". . . Though he does not attempt to deal with the rabbinic dietary code, it would splendidly confirm his central thesis. . . . From the prohibition of a kid in its mother's milk, the rabbis extrapolate a global separation of meat from dairy foods, involving separate dishes and pots and pans for meat and dairy meals and separate eating surfaces. If more than a sixty-fourth part of meat should accidently fall into a pot of dairy food, or vice versa, the food must be discarded, for opposed realms have been mingled, the sustaining substance of mammalian life and flesh of a slaughtered animal have been confounded, an ontological hybrid has been made. . . .

"Exponents of a culture that tended to see the world in securely defined hierarchies, the biblical legislators limited edibility chiefly to those creatures that seemed to fit safely into the category of classification, excluding . . . everything in the zoological realm that seemed in any way dissonant with the principle of ordered, shaped creation, everything that roused dim uneasy recollections of primordial chaos and void of which God called the world into being.

"In this connection, the initially puzzling invocation of the exodus at the end of the dietary code is thematically apt. . . . Out of a shapeless swarm of slaves—who . . . yearn nostalgically for the fleshpots of Egypt—God gave Israel the coherence and identity of a covenanted people. The process of liberation . . . is completed only with the acceptance of the Law. Both the world and the nation come into being through the establishment of a lawful hierarchy. The Hebrew aspiration to resemble God by making man holy is a staggering spiritual project, for the object of emulation is, after all, ultimately unknowable; at best, only certain of his attributes can be inferred from the revelations. . . . Perhaps this is why the system of laws, through which holiness is to be realized must be in many respects enigmatic, proceeding with a logic that is often hidden and sometimes ungraspable.

". . . In regard to the laws regulating diet, cult, dress and sex, it is an advance in understanding to see them . . . not primarily as a response to pragmatic pressures of the environment or as direct, quasi-allegorical expressions of spiritual concepts but as interrelated, internally coherent systems for ordering the world. The one great danger in this way of conceiving the function and meaning of the traditional laws is the temptation to reduce all biblical injunctions . . . to a single elegant common denominator. The tradition itself is more various, more interestingly contradictory for that (Robert Alter).[4]

BLOOD AND FAT—ALTAR, YES/KOSHER, NO

"Blood and fat symbolize opposite extremes. The blood contains the active life force of the animal and the fat symbolizes its inactive physical existence. The same qualities are essential elements of the makeup of human beings, and as such, they can be offered on the Altar as a sign of Man's devotion and commitment. However, it is important for man to avoid incorporating animal qualities within himself. Thus, he is forbidden to eat the symbols of these qualities" (Samson Raphael Hirsch).[5]

✤

POLITICAL SYMBOLISM— THE GREAT PRETENDER

"Why does Moses compare Rome to the swine? Just as a swine when it crouches puts forth its hoofs as if to say, 'I am clean,' so the wicked kingdom steals and grabs, while pretending to be setting up courts of justice.

"So Esau for all forty years hunted married women, ravished them, and when he reached the age of forty, he presented himself to his father saying, 'Just as father got married at the age of forty, so I shall marry a wife at the age of forty'" (*Genesis Rabbah*).

"The exegesis . . . identifies Esau with Rome. The roundabout link with Esau's taking a wife passes through the territory of Roman duplicity. Whatever the government does, it claims to do in the public interest. But it has no public interest at all. Esau for his part spent forty years pillaging women and then . . . pretends, to his father, to be upright" (Jacob Neusner).[6]

THE TEMPLE WILL RISE AND THE PIG WILL BE KOSHER

"The Midrash explains that the four non-kosher animals mentioned in [Leviticus 11] symbolize the four kingdoms that persecuted and enslaved the people of Israel in ancient times: Egypt, Babylon, Greece, and Rome. The fourth of these is associated with the pig, symbolizing the leaders of Rome who committed the most abominable crimes while assuming an air of uprightness and piety. . . . Nevertheless, the Midrash concludes (Vayikra Rabbah, 13) this empire will ultimately pay tribute to Hashem by rebuilding His temple, long after having destroyed it. The very name 'chazir,' pig, alludes to this return, for the verb 'chozair' means to return or give back. As Rabbeinu Bachya further explains, . . . Hashem will one day return the pig to its original purity" (Elie Munk).[7]

NOTES

1. *The Works of Philo*, "Special Laws," part 4, p. 626.
2. Ibid., pp. 626–627.

3. *Guide*, part 3, 26:509.

4. Alter, "A New Theory of Kashrut," pp. 46–48.

5. Munk, *Vayikra*, p. 24.

6. Jacob Neusner, *The Midrash: An Introduction* (Northvale, NJ: Jason Aronson Inc., 1990), pp. 156–157.

7. Munk, *Vayikra*, pp. 106–107.

7

Ecology

MORAL PURPOSE OF THE WORLD

"Hirsch's main thesis sounds like an introduction to a modern book on ecology. If we assume that there is order, design, and purpose in nature, then the needless felling of a tree is contrary to the original divine plan. Although man is endowed with claims upon nature, he is obliged to use them responsibly, for the improvement of man or for nature. For this reason, nature was given to man 'to till it and tend it.' This implies a privilege and an obligation. By employing the bounties of nature properly 'nature itself finds its appointed purpose promoted.' . . . By his work on it [the earth], man raises its purely physical nature into playing a part in the sphere of moral purpose of the world.

"Heedless destruction implies man's arrogance in proclaiming himself absolute master of the

world. By such acts he displays contempt for nature and disregard for God, who created it. Hirsch,
therefore, takes the prohibition against destroying
trees in a time of siege as the fundamental law of
all *hukkim*, accepting it in its widest connotation
and most far-reaching ramifications. It 'is the first
law which is opposed to your presumption against
things: Regard things as God's property and use
them with a sense of responsibility for wise pur-
poses.'

"This law against wanton destruction, therefore, constitutes the underlying principle upon
which man must relate himself to the realm of
nature. . . . He has to use nature judiciously, in-
telligently, and in accordance with the laws of the
Torah, because those laws, seemingly incompre-
hensible to man, are based on the infinite profound
understanding of nature possessed by its divine
creator" (Noah Rosenbloom).[1]

RESPECT FOR NATURE

"And if any Israelite or any stranger who resides
among them hunts down an animal or a bird that
may be eaten he shall pour out its blood and cover
it with earth" (Leviticus 17:13).

"The obligation to cover the blood of a dead animal applied only to birds and wild beasts but not
to domestic animals. Birds and wild beasts live by

the laws that God designed for them, independently of the needs or wishes of the human species. Domestic animals, by contrast, live mostly as the servants of man. Animals that are closely identified with nature should be accorded greater respect than those which have been subservient to human masters" (Recanti [thirteenth century]).[2]

THE NECESSITIES OF NATURE

"Moreover, Moses commands, that no man shall take of any dead carcass, or of any body that has been torn by wild beasts; partly because it is not fitting that man should share a feast with untameable beasts, so as to become a fellow reveller in their carnivorous festival; and . . . also, because it is proper to preserve that which has been preoccupied and seized beforehand, having a respect to the necessities of nature by which it has been seized" (Philo of Alexandria).[3]

THE BALANCE OF NATURE

"The list of prohibited creatures includes mainly carnivores. . . . [T]he bias against carnivores gives us a strong clue to scriptural preferences. . . . For when we come to animals we find . . . that the only ones permitted as human food are plant-eaters, herbivores. And even these are restricted to ruminants. . . .

". . . Herbivores . . . are not the only mammals that have been domesticated by human-kind. Dogs, the oldest sharers of our campfires, are meat-eaters and some peoples raise them for the reputed delicate taste of their flesh. Cats [and] [b]ears have been known to live with people, too. In theory, these gentle carnivores could be raised as sources of meat: in practice, it rarely works. The reason is an ecological one; many more herbivores can be kept than carnivores. To understand this, we need a short course in plant-eaters versus meat-eaters.

"The food chain that results in most human food begins with producers, green plants that trap a little of the sunlight on them, and use solar energy to grow more plant material. . . . Animals that eat plants are primarily consumers . . . these herbivores, are incapable of using sunlight directly, but must obtain their energy and matter from the plant they eat. Being a consumer is no energy bargain; no more then a tenth of the energy stored in the plant can be converted into a flesh of a consumer, and the actual efficiency of energy use is often much less. The inefficiency is ineluctable, built into the chemistry of living matter.

"Great masses of green land plants are required to support relatively small herds of herbivores. There are subtler reasons than feeding for this difference in numbers: the oxygen we inhale is a plant product and the carbon dioxide that is garbage to us is taken from our breaths into the energy-trapping machinery of plants. . . . If all the animals suddenly disappeared, the surface of our blue and green earth would change little, since only a few plants depend on animals for their pollination. Without plants almost all animal life would be gone.

"Carnivores, animals that eat other animals, are secondary consumers. They are fewer in number than the primary consumers they eat . . . being a consumer is inefficient. . . . [L]ess than 10 percent of the flesh of a primary consumer can be converted into that of a secondary consumer. And since energy is lost at each level of consumption, it follows that carnivores that eat other carnivores must either be small or few.

"For people, it makes ecological sense not to eat carnivores. Their flesh. . . . is energy expensive. Their meat is at least a hundred times dearer than the plants that originally trapped the rays of the sun.

"Of all foods, plants are the cheapest to eat. Indeed, most people in the world are vegetarians for most of their lives—not owing to religious belief but for lack of access to meat or lack of money to buy it. . . . Yet few Westerners are vegetarians by choice. If we can afford meat, we buy it. . . .

". . . [H]uman beings cannot digest grass; the nutrients within each cell of grass are locked behind a wall that our digestive juices cannot penetrate. These woody walls are composed of cellulose. . . . With few exceptions, no animal can break cellulose into the nutritious sugars of which it consists. How, then, can cows eat grass? Listen to the country-music stations that carry commodity prices and other news of interest to farmers: as often as not they also carry commercials for rumen bacteria. These bacteria inhabit the digestive tracts of animals, like cows, that are equipped with special pouches of rumens, where they digest cellulose into its constituent sugars. Once the cell walls of cellulose have been digested, nutrients inside the plant cells become accessible to the cow's digestive system. . . . Digestion of cellulose is not easy, even for a cow. As its jaws move from side to side, a cow grinds its food more thoroughly than the most fastidious hygienist. Grass is milled into fine particles, which present many surfaces that can be attacked by bacteria. The pouch that contains these bacteria, the rumen, is a large chamber filled by many gallons of fermenting food. When a cow chews its cud, it is chewing a mass of food brought up from its rumen to be milled and mixed again by another grinding. A cow rewards its bacterial helpers by providing a home for them. . . . Our reward, as meat eaters, is to derive the benefit of their work and the cow's work while still refraining from disturbing the general balance of nature.

". . . Carnivores . . . for all their imposing and dangerous appearances . . . lead precarious lives. Whereas herbivores may be 'harvested' by human beings and other predators in large numbers, any threat to the reproducing population of carnivores is serious. When we hunt animals for food, we increase the risk of reducing their numbers beneath the critical level at which a population of beasts can sustain itself. . . . Scripture protects them by banning their use as food. Among mammals only the most efficient herbivores, ruminants, are suitable sources of meat" (Newtol Press).[4]

SAVE THE TIGER

"Conservationists warn that the estimated 5,000 tigers left in the wild around the world could be gone in a few years. The poaching for their skins and body parts for their believed medicinal and sexual powers threatens some of the world's most beautiful and exotic animals.

"Three of the eight tiger subspecies are now extinct. Siegfried and Roy, the Las Vegas-based magic and wild animal act, have more tigers [38] on their estate than all the wild tigers in China [30]. In India, home of 60 percent of the world's remaining tigers, the country's tiger population plunged almost 15 percent between the 1989 and 1993 census."[5]

A LESSON FROM NOAH'S ARK

"Of every clean animal you shall take seven pairs, males and their mates, and of every animal which is not clean two, a male and its mate" (Genesis 7:2).

"Because they are non-predatory but are the prey of the carnivores, their species would have been exterminated altogether if he had not more of them in the ark" (Hizekuni [French, thirteenth century]).[6]

(An alternative explanation is that the carnivores would have starved.)

SAVING THE GENUS

"However, no animal from the herd or from the flock shall be slaughtered on the same day with its young" (Leviticus 22:28).

"If it is necessary to slaughter an animal for food, at least the cow and the calf should not be killed together, in order to demonstrate that man is not intent on destroying the genus of the animal. Therefore, he retains one to procreate its species as compensation for killing the other" (Abarbanel).[7]

REASON ALONE CANNOT EXPLAIN IT

"The notion of the preservation and enhancement of life as it is articulated in the Bible is by no means a sentimental one. It may seem to accord comfortably with our own ecological or humanitarian preference, but as a cultural logic it springs from an ultimately imponderable axiom. . . . For there is just no way of explaining . . . why life should be thought of as intrinsically good, a property to be reproduced and in normal peaceful circumstances to be held inviolate. Quite a few cultures before and since have thought otherwise, and the dissemination of practices like infanticide, ritual murder, human sacrifice, geronticide, and suicide suggests that very different conclusions could be drawn by civilized people about what attitude to adopt toward this trying, inscrutable, evanescent experience of life to which we are born and which is born all around us" (Robert Alter).[8]

NOTES

1. Rosenbloom, *Tradition*, pp. 318–319.
2. Chill, *Mitzvoth*, pp. 206–207.
3. *The Works of Philo*, "Special Laws," part 4, p. 627.
4. Newtol Press, "Kosher Ecology," *Commentary*, February 1985, pp. 56–58.
5. John Ward Anderson, "Poachers Felling World's Tigers, Rhinos," *Washington Post*, November 29, 1994, pp. A1, A18.
6. Menahem Kasher, *Encyclopedia of Biblical Interpretation—A Millennial Anthology*, Volume 2: *Genesis*, trans. Harry Freedman (New York: American Biblical Encyclopedia Society, 1955), p. 21.
7. Chill, *Mitzvoth*, p. 274.
8. Alter, "A New Theory of Kashrut," p. 51.

8

Ethic

MAN IS NOT JUST AN ANIMAL

"Only the flesh with the life thereof, which is the blood thereof, shall we not eat" (Genesis 9:24).

After man is specifically permitted to eat meat, he is instructed that he is not just a meat-eating animal. As anyone who has watched wildlife specials on public broadcasting has seen, the characteristic of carnivores is that the tearing of limbs and the eating and drinking of blood often precede the death of their victims. The animals have not made a decision to be cruel; it is just the value-free operation of nature. As for man, who stands midway between the natural and the divine, his way of eating must be sharply distinguished from the way of the natural world.

❧

THE BLOOD OF LIFE

"[T]he restriction was of a twofold nature. It firstly forbade . . . cutting a limb from a live animal—a barbarous practice common among primitive races; and secondly, the blood must not on any account be eaten, since it is the seat of life. The double prohibition . . . is the basis of most of the rules of Jewish slaughter of animals" (J. H. Hertz).[1]

A UNIQUE PRACTICE

"According to Berkeley Professor Jacob Milgrom, whose essay "The Biblical Dietary Laws as an Ethical System" put me on the road to kashrut, 'surprisingly, none of the Israel's neighbors possessed this absolute and universally binding blood prohibition. [M]an has a right to nourishment, not to life. Hence the blood, which is a symbol of life, must be drained, returned to the universe, to God.' [T]he unique practice of draining the blood from every piece of meat consumed over thousands of years has had a profoundly moral impact. It produced an extraordinary antipathy to blood among Jews. One example, in addition to the uniquely low incidence of violence among Jews, has been the virtual nonexistence of hunting among Jews" (Dennis Prager).[2]

RITUAL SLAUGHTER

"[T]he natural food of man consists of vegetables and the flesh of animals. . . . As necessity occasions the eating of animals, the commandment was intended to bring about the easiest death in an easy manner. . . . In order that death come about more easily, the condition was imposed that the knife should be sharp" (Maimonides).[3]

The Process

The *shochet* uses a knife that must be smoother and sharper than a surgical knife. The knife blade must be perfect, without the least perceptible nick. He cuts across the neck of the animal or fowl by moving the knife in a single swift and uninterrupted sweep. The cut severs the main arteries, rending the animal unconscious and permitting the blood to be drained from the body.

Objection has sometimes been raised that the process is cruel [*shechita* is banned in Switzerland]. However, the process, according to scientific opinion, brings about instant death with the least pain. The severance of the carotid arteries and the jugular vein by one swift movement results in the immediate loss of consciousness.[4]

Nonritual Slaughtering

On reaching the slaughterhouse, the broiler chickens are shackled by their legs to a moving line. Their heads and necks are dragged through an electrically charged water bath to stun the birds. The moving line then takes the birds to an automatic neck cutter. The birds are then bled before entering a scalding tank. Scalding makes the plucking easier.

Many chickens are still alive when entering the scalding tank. One study found nearly 25 percent of the birds were conscious on entering the scalding tank. The overwhelming majority of the broilers do not have their necks cut efficiently. Adequate neck cutting is opposed by the poultry industry on the basis it would cause problems for the automatic disembowelment of the birds.[5]

THE SHOCHET

A Learned and a Pious Man

"The one who slaughters the animal, the *Shochet*, must be carefully chosen. He must not only slaughter the animal according to Jewish law but is obliged to examine its internal organs to make certain the animal is not diseased. Among non-Jews such positions in slaughterhouses are held, for the most part, by the lowest element of society—tough, crude men. With Jews it is otherwise. The *Shochet* must be both a learned and pious man. He must pass an examination attesting to his thorough knowledge of the laws. . . . He must be a man of piety and is obliged to recite a blessing[6] before he executes his duties, ever mindful that this whole process is a 'divine concession.' Thus he is prevented from being brutalized by the manner of his work. . . . Thus, *shechita* teaches reverence for life" (Samuel Dresner).[7]

A Kindly Killer

"Several chasidim complained to the Sadagurer that the shochet in their town was a miserly and unfriendly person. The Rabbi exclaimed, 'Do you eat meat from his shechita?' The chasidim got the message and no one purchased meat.

"The shochet came to complain to the Rabbi, 'Where does it say that a shochet has to be friendly?' The Rabbi replied: 'We find in the Talmud that some persons are born with a passion for shedding blood. One becomes a murderer, the second, a soldier, and the third, a shochet. The question arises: "Why do we make use of meat from an animal killed by a man who is like a murderer?"

"'The answer is the shechita laws have been formulated to prevent brutal treatment to animals. A shochet should have a good heart, notwithstanding his love for the shedding of animal's blood. If he is kind to his fellow-men, he may be trusted to slaughter in a mild manner. But, if he is unkind, he is in truth a near-murderer, who cannot be trusted to observe the kind methods of killing animals prescribed by the Law'" (*The Hasidic Anthology*).[8]

✤

THE CASE OF FISH

The Absence of Ritual

"There are no laws governing the killing of fish. If shechita was merely a religious ritual and not an ethical system, there would be laws for the killing of all kosher animals. But no such law exists in the case of fish—there is no kosher salmon or flounder as there is kosher beefsteak or lambchop. The reason is that unlike land animals which can be killed in any number of painful ways, there is only one way to kill a fish, by taking it out of the water. . . . Moreover, the nervous system of a fish is so much more primitive than that of a mammal that preoccupation with painless ways is unnecessary" (Dennis Prager).[9]

Unsportsmanlike Conduct

"Eels are still skinned alive, cod is crimped, and lobsters are boiled unpithed. It is remarkable that Jews did not kill animals for sport. Fish had to be netted. Mr. William Radcliffe in his book, *Fishing*

From Earliest Times, blames Jews for lacking the sporting spirit. They caught fish by net; they did not play them with the rod. This is perfectly true. The word 'hook' occurs in the Bible only as a metaphor of cruelty, or as an instrument used by foreigners" (H. Lowe).[10]

❧

A MOTHER'S PAIN

Cow and Calf; Ewe and Lamb

"However, no animal from the herd or from the flock shall be slaughtered on the same day with its young" (Leviticus 22:28).

"For in these cases animals feel very great pain, there being no difference regarding this pain between man and other animals. For the love and the tenderness of a mother for her child is not consequent upon reason, but upon the activity of the imaginative faculty which is found in most animals just as it is found in man" (Maimonides).[11]

"Hirsch points to the specific moral and educational value of these laws for man. They were designed to ennoble his feelings and make him sensitive to the plight of every creature. Disregard for the suffering of nonhuman creatures may result in insensitivity to the agony of human beings: 'The boy who, in crude joy, finds delight in the convulsions of an injured beetle or the anxiety of suffering animals will soon be dumb toward human pain'" (Noah Rosenbloom).[12]

Save the Mother—Save the Child

"You shall not take the mother bird with the young. You shall let the mother bird go . . ." (Deuteronomy 22:6–7).

Think of the Bird

"For in general the eggs which the bird has sat and the young that need their mother are not fit to be eaten. If then the mother is let go . . . she will not be pained by seeing that the young are taken away. In most cases, this will lead people to leave everything alone, for what may be taken in most cases is not fit to be eaten. If the law takes into consideration these pains . . . in the case of beasts and birds, what will be the case in regard to the individuals of the human species . . ." (Maimonides).[13]

Think of the Man

"The reason for the prohibition of slaying the mother and the young on the same day as well as the ordinance of sending the mother is to eradicate cruelty and pitilessness from man's heart . . . not that God had pity on the mother bird or the mother of the young. Were that the case, God would have completely forbidden *shechita*. But the real reason is to cultivate *in us* the quality of mercy . . .

since cruelty is contagious, as is well known from
the example of professional animal killers who
become hardened to human suffering. . . .

"These precepts regarding bird and beast are
not motivated by pity for the beast but are decrees
of the Almighty to cultivate good moral qualities in
man" (Nachmanides).[14]

✤

MILK AND MEAT

"You shall not boil a kid in its mother's milk" (Exodus 23:19, 34:26; Deuteronomy 14:21).

A Quality of Humanness

"The act implies extreme barbarism. The mitzvah
is placed in the same category as that of sending
away the mother bird. In both cases the quality of
humanism is stressed" (Ibn Ezra [1092–1167]).[15]

Separating Death from Life

"This concept is directly related to Judaism's ob-
session with separating death from life. Judaism
is the only religion in history which is preoccupied
with this life and virtually ignores the issue of life
after death. Compare normative Christianity with
its emphasis on the Crucifixion, Resurrection, the
Cross, and salvation after this life; compare Islam's

emphasis on the heavenly rewards . . . ; compare the Eastern religions' preoccupation with leaving, even denying, this world, this life and the self and entering Nirvana. . . .

"One proof of this explanation is that only milk producing animals may not be eaten with milk. We are allowed to eat fish and milk together because fish do not produce milk. Milk does not represent life with regard to fish, as it does with regard to mammals. Chickens, which do not produce milk, were not originally considered 'meat' and the Talmud itself noted that one of the great Talmudic rabbis, Rabbi Yosi Ha-G'lili, ate chicken with milk. As the tradition grew it came to include chicken with 'meat'" (Dennis Prager).[16]

Ungrateful and Callous

"Another 'reason' for the prohibition may be that the goat . . . generously and steadfastly provides man with the single most perfect food he possesses: milk. It is the only food which, by reason of its proper composition of fat, carbohydrate, and protein, can by itself sustain the human body. How ungrateful and callous we would be to take the child of an animal to whom we are so indebted and cook it in the very milk which nourishes us and is given to us so freely by its mother" (Abraham Joshua Heschel).[17]

A DOG'S REWARD

"You shall not eat any flesh that is torn by beasts of the field, you should cast it to the dogs" (Exodus 22:30).

"Dogs act as guardians of flocks of sheep and herds of cattle. The animal that falls prey is fed to the dogs as a reward for their efforts to protect the animals" (Ibn Ezra).[18]

DO NOT MUZZLE

"You shall not muzzle an ox when he is treading out the corn" (Deuteronomy 25:4).

"It is a refinement of cruelty to excite the animal's desire for food and to prevent its satisfaction.

"The claims of lower animals on human pity and consideration are characteristic of the Hebrew scriptures. . . . In the Decalogue, the animals that labor with and for man have their share of the Sabbath rest, and the produce of the fields during the Sabbatical year is to be for them as for the poor.

"The duty to our dumb friends has been strangely overlooked in most ethical systems. . . . Paul dismisses as idle sentimentalism the notion of man's duty to the animals. 'Is it for oxen that God careth?' he asks mockingly" (J. H. Hertz).[19]

WHY JEWS DON'T EAT SIRLOIN

"Jacob was left alone. And a man wrestled with him until the break of dawn. When he saw that he had not prevailed against him, he wrenched Jacob's hip at its socket, so that the socket of his hip was strained as he wrestled with him. . . . The sun rose upon him as he passed Penuel, limping on his hip. That is why the children of Israel to this day do not eat the thigh muscle that is on the socket of the hip, since Jacob's hip socket was wrenched at the thigh muscle" (Genesis 30:25–26, 32–33).

"The Torah relates that on the night before his confrontation with Esau, in which his thigh was injured, Jacob was left by himself. He was alone when he encountered the angel who engaged him in a struggle. How could his sons and the rest of his entourage have allowed him to remain alone all that night? In memory of this incident, we refrain from eating the thigh muscle to remind us that we must never permit a fellow Jew feel that he is alone in the world" (Hizekuni [French, thirteenth century]).[20]

CHEAP SNEAKERS ON YOM KIPPUR

"Rabbi Moses Isserles wrote: It is the custom to say to a person putting on a new garment, 'May you wear it out and get a new one.' There are some who write that one ought not to say this about shoes or clothing which are made from the skin of animals (even if unclean), for if that were the case, it would seem as though the animal were being killed to make a garment, and it is written, 'His tender mercies are over all His works.' Rabbi Mosses Isserles also wrote that he who is slaughtering an animal ought to recite the blessing [for doing something the first time] when he covers the blood of the animal, not when he slaughters it; for he is injuring a living thing. Therefore, how can a man put on shoes, a piece of clothing for which it is necessary to kill a living thing, on Yom Kippur, which is a day of grace and compassion?"[21]

NOTES

1. Hertz, *Pentateuch* 1:32.

2. Dennis Prager, "Should a Modern Jew Keep Kosher?" *Brandeis Bardin Institute Newsletter*, Spring 1980.

3. *Guide*, Part 3, 26:508–509.

4. *Encyclopaedia Britannica, Micropaedia*, 15th ed., 6:969.

5. John Davis, British Vegetarian Society, "Information Sheets," *Internet*, John@ port sveg.demon.coUK.

6. Unlike the procedure among Muslims, each animal doesn't require a separate prayer.

7. Dresner, "Their Meaning For Our Time," pp. 27–28.

8. Louis Newman, *The Hasidic Anthology* (New York: Schocken Paperbacks, 1968), p. 14.

9. Prager, "Should a Modern Jew Keep Kosher?"

10. Quoted in Dresner, "Their Meaning For Our Time," pp. 32–33.

11. *Guide*, part 3, 48:599.

12. Rosenbloom, *Hirsch*, p. 325.

13. *Guide*, part 3, 48:600.

14. Quoted in Leibowitz, *Studies in Leviticus*, pp. 208– 209.

15. Chill, *Mitzvoth*, p. 114.

16. Prager, " Should A Modern Jew Keep Kosher?"

17. Quoted in Dresner, "Their Meaning For Our Time," p. 101.

18. Chill, *Mitzvoth*, p. 93.

19. Hertz, *Pentateuch* 2:854.

20. Chill, *Mitzvoth*, p. 8.

21. Quoted in Shmuel Yosef Agnon, *Days of Awe* (New York: Schocken Books, 1965), pp. 200–201.

9

The Vegetarian
Challenge

LIGHT FARE

The Munch of Time

Dietary Restrictions

First Generation—Anything that is not kosher.
Second Generation—Anything that is not kosher, except Chinese food.
Third Generation—Anything with cholesterol.
Fourth Generation—Anything with meat in it and anything that was not organically grown.[1]

Vegetarianism from a Jewish Perspective

Orthodox

Vegans (vegetarians) exclude animal flesh (meat, poultry, fish and seafood) from their diet. They do not eat (eggs and dairy) or use animal products

137

(leather, silk, wool, violins [stuck together with animal glue, horsehair bow]). They usually eat no honey, and some also refuse to eat yeast products.

Ultra-Orthodox

Fruitarians are vegans who eat only foods that do not require the killing of the plant (apples are acceptable, but carrots are not).

Conservative

> Ovo-Lacto—A vegan who eats eggs and milk products. This is the most popular form of vegetarianism.
> Ovo—A vegan who eats eggs.
> Lacto—A vegan who eats milk products.

Reform

These are vegans who eat kosher.

A ROAD TO MORALITY OR A HIGHWAY TO HOLINESS

A Moral Compromise

"The major Jewish dietary laws rest on a single premise: *Eating meat is a moral compromise.* There is a difference between eating a hamburger and eating a bowl of cereal. . . . Our family, which for many years ate kosher meat, has gradually become vegetarian for a combination of religious, moral, and health reasons. We see it as an extension of the discipline and sensitivity inculcated by keeping kosher" (Harold Kushner).[2]

Reach for the Heights

"The new era [after the Flood] spelled the end of the vegetarian diet which had been in force from the creation. . . . Far from calming man's behavior, this diet had been powerless to prevent him from becoming cruel, egoistic, and perverse. Accordingly, a new orientation was now called for. It was part of a new method of moral training, which was to permit all of creation to raise itself up, progressively, to holiness. [See Moses Cordovero, Chapter 4 of this book.]

"Seen in this perspective, the authorization for eating meat is part of the universal uplifting of the spheres of creation to the heights of holiness" (Elie Munk).[3]

EATING MEAT VIOLATES
KOSHER JEWISH VALUES

"While Judaism emphasizes compassion for animals, animals today are raised for food under cruel conditions in crowded cells, where they are denied fresh air, exercise, and any emotional stimulation.

"While Judaism mandates us to be careful about preserving our health and our lives, flesh-centered diets have been linked to heart disease, several forms of cancer, and other diseases.

"While Judaism stresses that we are to share our bread with hungry people, over 70 percent of the grain grown in the United States is fed to animals destined for slaughter and twenty million people die annually because of hunger and its effects.

"While Judaism teaches . . . we are partners with God in preserving the world and in seeing that the earth's resource are properly used, flesh-centered diets require huge amounts of land, water, energy, and other resources and result in extensive pollution, soil erosion, and threats to tropical rain forests and other habitats.

"While Judaism stresses that we must seek and pursue peace and that violence results from unjust conditions, flesh-centered diets help to perpetuate widespread hunger and poverty and eventually lead to instability and war" (Richard H. Schwartz).[4]

COUNTERPOINTS

The Laws Abhor Cruel Treatment

The cruel treatment of animals, even nonkosher ones, violates Jewish laws ("tzar baalei chaim"—

causing pain to animals). Kosher-eaters are on the side of animal-rights groups as to the prevention of inhumane practices. Perhaps kosher certifications can go beyond *glat* (a more stringent level of physical examination that rejects animals whose lungs are not smooth) to *mercy-glat*, which would reject animals that were raised inhumanely. It won't satisfy everyone. The setting of standards may be difficult. Meat may be more expensive. The vegetarian still will not eat range-fed animals or veals raised with tender loving care.

How Much Flesh Makes a "Flesh Centered" Diet?

In the United States in 1991, the per capita annual consumption of all major food commodities (including fruits and vegetables) was 1,750 pounds. The red meat component (including 47 pounds of pork) was 112 pounds (6.4 percent). "Sugar Coated" more accurately characterizes the American diet. The sweetener component was 140 pounds (*Statistical Abstract of the U.S.—1993*).[5]

Is Vegetarian Synonymous with Good Health?

Kosher is not synonymous with healthy. A Jew who eats like a pig may be ritually correct but not particularly healthy. A Jew who eats a balanced diet that includes meat is not doing his body any harm. A vegetarian whose daily fare is Twinkies and Cokes is not a healthy individual. Vegans who eat the correct portions of grain and vegetables and throw in a bit of B_{12} can provide their bodies with adequate nutrition.

A vegetarian diet is not necessarily lower in fats and calories. A recent *Washington Post* survey tested the fat and caloric content of two sandwiches purchased from the Wall Street Deli, one of the many shops that offer a meat-free alternative. The vegetarian sub comes with avocado, Swiss and American cheese, sprouts, lettuce, tomatoes, peppers, onions, and mayonnaise and had 28 grams of fat, 663 calories; the roast beef sub came with lettuce, tomato, and mustard and had 8 grams of fat, 509 calories.[6]

Is There a Relationship between Meat-Eating and Hunger?

The argument that Americans shouldn't eat meat because millions in the "undeveloped world" are dying of hunger sounds like the admonition that children should finish their meals because people in China are starving. U.S. food grain stocks are now up to 650 million tons. During the major African drought, food aid requirements never totalled more than 40 million tons.

Despite the addition of a billion persons during the prior twelve years, more people enjoyed adequate nutrition in 1990 than ever before. Per capita crop production continued to increase, with important gains in such countries as India and China. Given the increase in food production and the breadth of the gains in a wide variety of countries and basic food staples, a higher proportion of the world's population had adequate food than ever before.[7]

The Planet Is Being Saved by High Tech Farming

Since the 1930s, the yield per acre of corn in the United States has risen from twenty-five bushels to as high as three hundred bushels per acre as a result of research that has produced better fertilizing methods and bred-in pesticides. The same is true of other food crops.

High yields are currently saving 10 million square miles (the land area of North America) of wildlife habitat from being plowed under for inefficient farming. Herbicides make possible conservation tillage that minimizes soil erosion. Pesticies, by lowering the cost of fruits and vegetables, cut cancer risks.[8]

Correlation Not Causation

There is a relationship between war and instability and hunger and starvation. But it is the former that causes the latter—witness Somalia, Ethopia, Rwanda, Bosnia, and the former Soviet Union. Is the Middle East not yet at peace because one side is hungrier than the other?

GARDEN OF EDEN—A VEGETARIAN PARADISE

"God said, 'See, I give you every seed-bearing plant that is upon all the earth, and every tree that has seed-bearing fruit; they shall be yours for food. And to all the animals on land, and to all the birds of the sky, and to everything that creeps on earth, in which there is the breath of life, [I give] all the green plants for food'" (Genesis 1:29).

Garden of Eden—A Model for the Laws of Kashrut

(This is a case in which what is "kosher" for a fruitarian is "not kosher" for Adam.)

"And the Lord God commanded the man saying 'Of every tree of the garden you are free to eat, but as for the tree of knowledge of good and bad, you must not eat of it; for as soon as you eat of it, you shall die'" (Genesis 2:16–17).

"With this prohibition the education of man for his moral, high Godly calling begins. It is the beginning of the history of mankind, and shows all following generations the path they are to tread. It is . . . not a so-called "reasonable prohibition" . . . but rather one which all human means of judgement speak against; taste, sight, appeal to imagination and mind are all in favor of eating the fruit. Of oneself one would never come to forbid it, and even after the prohibition no other reason for it could possibly have been found than the absolute will of God; accordingly it is a *hok* [divine statute] in *optima forma*. Furthermore, it is a dietary law, and it reached the one to whom it applied only by way of tradition, oral communication. . . . At every demand of God's law of morality every one of us still stands like the first human pair, before the tree of this knowledge and has to decide whether he will follow the voice of bodily sensuality, his own judgment and sense, and the wisdom of instinctive animal life, or conscious of his higher calling, the voice of God" (Samson Raphael Hirsch).[9]

🌱

FROM ADAM TO NOAH

A Vegetarian World

The garden represents the ideal. After the Flood, meat is explicitly permitted to Noah and his descendants, but with an emphatic ban on eating the life of the animal (its blood) together with meat. The draining of blood is seen as a symbolic gesture in the direction of vegetarianism, which is no longer feasible.

Why Did Vegetarians Become Violent?

"In the end the prohibition against eating meat was misinterpreted by humanity and led to disastrous consequences—the Flood. People began to think that the reason they were forbidden to eat meat was because man and the animal were on the same level. This led to the conclusion that man is no more responsible for his actions than are the animals. Such a belief naturally led to moral degeneracy and ultimately to the Flood. After the Flood, the prohibition against meat was lifted so that man could realize their superiority over the animal kingdom and their corresponding greater degree of moral superiority" (Elie Munk).[10]

Madonna and k.d. lang

News item, *Washington Post*, Febuary 4, 1995: "Madonna and k. d. lang are to star in an anti-meat campaign sponsored by People for Ethical Treatment of Animals."

k.d. lang, Pop superstar, has been described as part Elvis Presley and part Barbra Streisand. Her off-stage life has been described as follows: "It is the perfect world. Lang has just finished nuzzling with Hannah and Arthur, the goats, and bringing a bucket of something wet, grayish and disgusting to Gracie, the very dirty pig."[11]

An Alternative Reading

The Killing of the First Animal

"And the Lord God made garments of skins for Adam and his wife and clothed them" (Genesis 3:21).

The gesture by God is interpreted as a merciful act after the divine punishment of expulsion from the garden.

The Second Oldest Profession

Adam was a farmer. Cain was a farmer. Abel was a sheepherder. Why do people herd sheep?

Abel's lambs are more pleasing to God than Cain's fruits.

"Abel became a keeper of sheep and Cain became a tiller of the soil. In the course of time, Cain brought an offering to the Lord from the fruit of the soil. And Abel for his part brought the choicest of the firstlings of his flock. The Lord paid heed to Abel's offering" (Genesis 4:2–4).

The Meat Business Grows

"Adal bore Jabal, he was the ancestor of those who dwell in their tents and amidst the herds" (Genesis 4:20).

GOD'S THOUGHTS AFTER NOAH'S SACRIFICE OF MEAT

"Then Noah built an altar to the Lord and taking of every clean bird, he offered burnt offerings on the altar. The Lord smelled the pleasing odor and the Lord said to himself, *'Never again will I doom the earth because of man, since the devising of man's mind are evil from his youth* nor will I ever again destroy every living being as I have done'" (Genesis 8:20–21).

Is the statement that "the devising of man's mind is evil from his youth" indicative of a degeneration of man that would require a concession to eat meat?

Some Commentaries[12]

"After the flood the natural balance in man was weakened, his intelligence no longer illumined his path from the days of his youth onward, that he might conquer his evil propensities" (Sforno).

"Evil entered the heart of Adam from the time he acquired the knowledge of good and evil—'evil from his youth' meaning from the youth of Adam" (Luzzato).

"In the youth [infancy] of the human race his intelligence and discernment were undeveloped, therefore, his corruption was complete and absolute. Now, however, that period has passed and his intelligence is more developed such an absolute punishment is no longer necessary" (Abarbanel).

"Before the flood, the heart of man is described as 'solely evil, all the time' (Genesis 6:5). After the flood, man is only rotten as a child" (Isaac Arama).

"The Hebrew word for youth, *naar*, originally meant to shake off. Youth views self-control and obedience to duty as an irksome yoke which their natures, striving for independence, shake off. But it is in this independence that the whole morality of man has its roots. God chose Israel because it was the most stiff-necked of nations. Once this obstinacy and independence of spirit has been directed into use in the direction for good, this independence would be used to preserve and stick to the good and right" (Samson Raphael Hirsch).

EATING MEAT IS A BLESSING

"God blessed Noah and his sons, and said to them, 'Be fertile and increase and fill the earth. The fear and the dread of you shall be upon all the beasts of the earth and upon all the birds of the sky— everything which the earth is astir—and upon all the fish of the sea; they are given into your hand. Every creature that lives shall be yours to eat; as with the green grasses, I give you all these'" (Genesis 9:1–4).

Man's Stomach Predisposed to Meat

"Our digestive tracts are predisposed to meat. As omnivores, we have guts that are intermediate in length between the long intestines of herbivores and the short one of carnivores. And length aside, the chemicals in our gut also favor meat" (Newtol Press).[13]

Unpopular Laws Are Unenforceable

"God's essential nature as a sustainer of life does call into question our human propensity, or perhaps virtual necessity, to live off other life. But if the authors of the Levitical code cast even a fleeting glance at the possibility of a vegetarian solution, they must have realized it would be popularly unacceptable and perhaps nutritionally and economically imprudent. For an unfeasible renunciation, they substituted an elaborate system of restriction" (Robert Alter).[14]

The Growth of McDonald's

The number-one growth item in American restaurants in 1994 was burgers. McDonald's is having trouble opening up restaurants fast enough to satisfy the craving for burgers of the "grain centered" people of the Far East.

A "Contented Heart" or a "Craving Heart"?

"When the Lord enlarges your territory as he has promised you and you say, 'I shall eat some meat,' for you have the urge to eat meat, you may eat whenever you wish. . . . [Y]ou may slaughter any of the cattle or sheep that the Lord gives you, as I have instructed you; and you may eat to your heart's content in your settlements . . . " (Deuteronomy 12:20–22).

Commentators Troubled by Killing

"Why ritual slaughter? Far more appropriate for man not to eat meat. Torah requires a troublesome and inconvenient procedure in the hope that the bother and annoyance of the whole procedure will restrain him from a strong and uncontrollable desire for meat" (*Keli Yakar*).[15]

When asked if he was a vegetarian for health reasons, Isaac Bashevis Singer replied, "Yes, for the chicken's health."

VEGETARIANISM AS AN ECHO
OF THE FUTURE

"The free movement of the moral impulse to establish justice for animals generally and the claim of their rights from mankind are hidden in a natural psychic sensibility in the deep layers of the Torah. In the ancient value system of humanity, . . . before nations were differentiated into distinct speech forms, the moral sense had risen to a point of demanding justice for animals. 'The first man had not been allowed to eat meat' (Sanhedrin, 59b). . . . But when humanity, in the course of its development, suffered a setback and was unable to bear the great light of its illumination, its receptive capacity being impaired, it was withdrawn from the fellowship with other creatures, whom it excelled with firm spiritual superiority. Now, it became necessary to confine the concern with justice and equity to mankind, so that the divine fire, burning with a very dim light, might be able to warm the heart of man, which has cooled off as a result of the many pressures of life. The changes in thought and disposition . . . required the moral duty be concentrated on the plane of humanity alone. But the thrust of the ideals in the course of development will not always remain confined. Just as the democratic aspiration will reach outward, the general intellectual and moral perfection, 'when man shall no longer teach his brother to know the Lord, for they will know Me, small and great alike' (Jeremiah 31:34), so will the hidden yearning to act justly toward animals emerge as the proper time. What

prepares the ground for this state is the commandments, those intended specifically for this area of
concern.

"There is indeed a hidden reprimand between
the lines of the Torah in the sanction to eat meat,
for it is only after 'you will say I will eat meat, because you lust after eating meat then you may
slaughter and eat.'. . . The only way you would be
able to overcome your inclination would be through
moral struggle, but the time for this conquest is
not yet. . . . The long road of development, after
man's fall, also needs physical exertion, which will
at times require a meat diet, which is a tax for
passage to a more enlightened epoch. . . . Human
beings also acted thus in their most justified wars,
which were incumbent on them as a transition to
a higher general state. . . .

"The commandments, therefore, came to regulate the eating of meat, in steps that will take us
to the higher purpose. The living beings we are
permitted are limited to those that are most suitable to the nature of man. The commandment to
cover the blood of an animal or bird captured while
hunting focuses on a most apparent and conspicu-
ous iniquity. These creatures are not fed by man,
they impose no burden on him to raise and develop
them. The verse . . . involves the acknowledgement
of a shameful act. This is the beginning of moral
therapy. . . . These efforts will bear fruit and in the
course of time people will be educated. The silent
protest will in time be transformed into a mighty
shout and it will triumph in its objective. The regulations of slaughter . . . to reduce the pain regis-

ters a reminder that . . . they are not automatons devoid of life. . . . What is inscribed in such letters on rolls of parchment will be read in the future, when the human heart will be conditioned for it. The feelings of the animal, the sensitivity to its family attachment implied in the rule not to slaughter an ox or sheep 'with its young on the same day' . . . and . . . the caution against callous violation of the moral sense . . . in the breakup of family im plied in the directive concerning a bird's nest, to let the mother bird go before taking the young[:] . . . all these join in a mighty demonstration against the general inequity that stirs every heart. . . . The divine protest could not extend to man's right over animal raised by him, until a much later time Then concern will even be shown for the taste of food eaten by the tilling animal, expressing a permanent spirit of compassion and an explicit sense of justice, 'Oxen and asses that till the soil will eat their fodder savored with spices, and winnowed with shovel and fan to remove the chaff' (Isaiah, 30:24).

"The prohibition of eating fat comes to us . . . in a subdued call. If, by necessity, to strengthen your prowess, you slaughter an animal, which you raised by your exertion, do not indulge in this to satisfy the vulgar craving that lusts for fat. . . . When the savage luxury of eating fat and blood . . . is forbidden, it takes away the worst element of this cruel gluttony. The impact of this provision will become apparent in the full maturing of culture that is due to come in the future. . . .

"The mixing of meat and milk . . . is pervaded altogether with the oppression of life. . . . Milk which serves so naturally to feed the tender child, . . . was not created so as to stuff with it the stomach, when you are so hard and cruel to eat meat. The tender child has a prior and more natural right than you.

"Just as the rule to cover the blood extends the sway of 'You shall not murder' to the domain of the animal, and the prohibition of mixing meat and milk . . . extends the injunctions, 'You shall not rob,' and 'You shall not oppress,' so does the rule against eating meat of an animal killed by another animal or one that died by itself extend the duty to offer help and visit the sick to the animal kingdom: be compassionate at least on the unfortunate ones, if your heart is insensitive to the healthy and the strong.

"When this seed is planted in the thick earth of the field blessed by the Lord, it will bear its fruit. It is necessary for its cultivation to join all these sensibilities into a natural center so that the echo released shall not be the voice of the weaklings, of ascetics and timid spirits, but the firm and joyous voice of life" (Rabbi Abraham Isaac Kook, First Chief Rabbi of Israel).[16]

THE PASCHAL LAMB

"According to most halachic authorities, when the Temple is rebuilt, all Jewish men will be obligated to partake of the paschal lamb with their families."[17]

VEGETARIANISM AS AN ECHO
OF THE PAST

"The dietary laws push the children of Israel back in the direction of the original 'vegetarianism' of the pristine and innocent garden of Eden. Although not all flesh is forbidden, everything that is forbidden is flesh. Thus, any strict vegetarian, one could say, never violates the Jewish dietary laws. Yet though he does not violate them, one could not say that he follows them. For only unknowingly does he not violate them, and more to the point, he refrains *indiscriminately*, that is, without regard to the distinctions among the kinds of living things that might or might not be edible. In this sense, the strict vegetarian, though he rejects the Noachic permission to eat meat, shares exactly the indiscriminate Noachic grouping-together of all the animals and its concentration only on the blood, which is life.

"But why, one may still ask, does not the Torah institute other dietary laws that push all the way back to vegetarianism, reversing altogether the Noachic permission to eat meat? Is not vegetarianism the biblical ideal, if the restricted meat diet of *Leviticus* is really nothing more than a compromise, a recognition that it is too much to expect these stiff-necked human beings to go back to nuts and berries. Perhaps, we were wrong to see the Noachic dispensations as merely concessive, a yielding to Noah's (and mankind's) prideful bloody-mindedness. Perhaps, looking again, we can see here something elevating.

"Noah, the incipiently civilized man, having spent time in close quarters with the animals, figured out, as a result, his human difference; he learned that he was more than just king of the animals. He learned that he was ambiguous because godlike animal, both capable and in need of self-restraint through the rule of law, and also open to the intelligible order of multiform world. The result was the new world order after the Flood. To mark his self conscious separation from the animals, man undertakes to eat them, to acknowledge his own godlikeness, man accepts the prohibition of homicide (Genesis 9:3–4, 9:6).

"Eating meat may indeed be part and parcel—albeit a worrisome one—of our humanization. This humanization can only be achieved at some cost to the harmony of the whole. The price is noted with regret, but it must be paid. And it might be worth paying, in order to keep the humans ever mindful of the forms and distinctions that are the foundation of the world. It might be superhuman or (as some would argue) more godlike for humans to renounce their rational difference from the animals and affirm by an act of choice the prehuman instinctive diet of fruit and seed; but it would also be less than human. The Levitical dietary laws fit the human animal in his distinctive uprightness; celebrating the principle of rational separation, they celebrate not only man's share in rationality but also his openness to the mystery of intelligibility yet embodied form.

". . . There is motion toward the source of that

order, toward that which was highest over all. The Noachic covenant with all flesh had denied in a way the dignity of flesh as variously formed and active, reserving it only for blood. . . . 'Do not eat the high' says the Noachic law on meat. The Levitical permissions and prohibitions say the reverse 'Do not eat the detestable.' The clean is to be incorporated. The legal distinction between clean and unclean is somehow higher than the natural principle of living and nonliving. . . .

"There is elevation in these restrictions. The clean and the holy, once far removed, are incorporated into daily life. Eating the clean, under laws given by the Holy one, symbolizes the sanctification of eating" (Leon Kass).[18]

FORBIDDEN FRUIT

"And when you shall come into the land . . . you shall count the fruit as forbidden, three years shall it be forbidden to you, it should not be eaten. And in the fourth year all the fruit of the land shall be holy for giving praise to the Lord" (Leviticus 19:23–24).

ELEVATING THE BODY

"All the duties of Judaism are for *man*, a physical and restricted creature. And for this reason there are also certain laws that are only for the bestial desires of man. That is not negative in any sense because, since man is imperfect, there must be a real relation to sin, 'You must stoop to him if you want to elevate him.'

"This way is not a necessary evil but an ideal in itself. In a more general sense, the aim of man is not to do holy duties and to be an angel on earth. Man's task is to reveal God's being in the lower world—and that is done by elevating the base and low elements and exalting them. [T]he lowest elements in the world are, essentially and originally, of the highest sources, because only very holy and great souls can enliven mean creations, and the task of man is to bring these souls back to their exalted origin.

"And so man has not to elevate his soul, because it is already high without man's efforts; his task is to elevate his body, his intellect, his desires. The human being is to give all his essence to God, but not by elevating his mind to higher subjects and converting his desires into the desire of God. The real way is higher; to find God in all these thoughts and desires; to be a whole man—but to a higher degree."

Adin Steinsaltz[19]

NOTES

1. Peter Hochstein, *Up from Seltzer—A Handy Guide to 4 Jewish Generations* (New York: Workman Publishing, 1981).

2. Harold Kushner, *To Life* (Boston: Little Brown and Co, 1993), pp. 56–57.

3. Munk, *Genesis*, pp. 204 205.

4. Richard Schwartz, preface to *Judaism and Vegetarianism*, 2d ed. (Marblehead, MA: Micah Publications, 1988).

5. Table 218, 219, pp. 142–143.

6. Carol Sugarman and Sandra Evan, "'Low Fat': Heavy on Promises, Light on Proof," *Washington Post*, March 15, 1995, p. A7.

7. Dennis Avery, *Global Food Progress: 1991*, in Stephen Moore, "So Much for Scarce Resources," *Public Interest*, Winter 1994, p. 102.

8. Dennis Avery, "Don't Worry, Eat and be Happy," *Wall Street Journal*, December 11, 1995, p. A12.

9. Rosenbloom, *Tradition*, p. 317.

10. Munk, *Vayikra*, p. 104.

11. Leslie Bennets, "k.d. Cuts It Close," *Vanity Fair*, August, 1993, p. 142.

12. *Encyclopedia of Biblical Interpretation* 2:49 for the first three commentaries; Munk, *Genesis*, p. 198, for the fourth; Sampson Raphael Hirsch, *The Pentateuch*, vol. 1 (Gateshead, England: Judaica Press Ltd., 1982), p. 166, for the fifth.

13. Press, "Kosher Ecology," pp. 56–58.

14. "A New Theory of Kashrut," p. 51.

15. *Keli Yakar*, in Chill, *Mitzvoth*, p. 400.

16. "Essay," in Ben Zion Bokser, ed., *Rabbi Abraham Isaac Kook*, trans. by editor (Mahwah, NJ: Paulist Press, 1978), pp. 317–321.

17. "Frequently Asked Questions on Soc.Culture. Jewish," *America Online*, Last Post: January 31, 1995, Part 4: Observance, Subject 6.9.

18. Leon Kass, excerpts from "Why the Dietary Laws?" *Commentary*, June 1994, pp. 46–47.

19. Adin Steinsaltz, "Human Holiness," in *The Strife of the Spirit* (Northvale, NJ: Jason Aronson Inc., 1988) pp. 40–41.

10

The Sanctification of the Ordinary

SEPARATE AND SANCTIFY

"I believe . . . [the dietary laws] embody and reflect a more or less true understanding not only of the problematic character of eating but, more significantly, of the nature of nature and of the place of man within the whole. They implicitly pay homage to the articulated order of the world and the dignity of life and living form; they incorporate into the act of eating an acknowledgement of the problematic character of eating as a threat to order, life and form, and they celebrate in gratitude and reverence the mysterious source . . . and its generous hospitality in providing food for both life and thought.

"The remarkable customs not only restrain and thwart the bad; they also commemorate the true and beckon the good. Finally the dietary laws of Leviticus commemorate the creation and the Creator and beckon us towards holiness. . . .

". . . We could say that *the* fundamental principle through which the world is created is *separation*. Creation is the bringing of order out of chaos by acts of separation. . . . [T]he word, 'divide or separate' (*badal*) occurs explicitly five times in the first chapter and . . . implicitly ten more times in the expression 'after its kind' which implies the separation of plants and animals into distinct and separable kinds.

Living things . . . are characterized . . . by having a proper place[,] . . . by having motion appropriate to their place . . . and by reproducing themselves according to their kind. . . . [T]hey also have the power of awareness—especially hearing . . . ; they can recognize the distinctions that are manifest in the world, and ultimately one of them—man—can understand those conveyed in speech. Finally, they are characterized by vulnerability, which may be what makes them in need of God's blessing.

". . . [T]he very last subject of the first chapter, before God's pronouncement that everything is very good, is the matter of food. After blessing man to be fruitful and multiply . . . and to have dominion over all life, God teaches man that dominion does not mean appropriation or exploitation. . . . The only instruction given to man, the ruler, created in the image of God is . . . about food—his and that of his subjects. . . . [T]hey are all to be vegetarian. . . .

"Beginning in the garden of Eden, the problem of eating and its regulation . . . receives prominent attention. . . . The need for dietary laws is, to start with, identical to the need for law in general, and laws to regulate conduct are very often heralded by or presented in terms of regulations of eating. Indeed, the Torah presents us with a series of stages in the development of the human race, leading up to the formation of the people of Israel, each of which is marked by a change in the diet, usually involving restrictions.

" . . . [A]t the beginning . . . man was a fruit eater allowed to eat of every tree of the garden—save one. . . . The expulsion from the garden is coupled with a shift from fruit to bread. . . . Men turn from gathering naturally available food (fruits) to toil —some cultivation of grain, itself in need of artful transformation before it becomes edible as bread.

"But civilization here proceeds in the absence of law. Men are left to their own devices and beginning with the fratricide of Cain, the whole earth becomes corrupt and violent—including also the animals [Genesis 6:12] by which we may understand that they became carnivorous. By the tenth generation, men are disordering . . . the created order with no respect for life or limb. The return through the Flood to the watery chaos of the beginning completes the chaos that life itself has wrought.

"The next and crucial stage, just after the Flood, is marked by the first law for all mankind and the first covenant between God and man. . . . God decides against blotting out and starting over; it would not do any good. Instead he chooses the way of the law. The covenant with Noah makes a concession to man's violence and carnivorousness, but only by bringing it somewhat under law.

"In becoming a creature under law, quasi-'political' man is decisively separated from the animal friends and relations, in the interest of elementary decency and justice in human life. For the Noachic law also for the first time prohibits murder and compels human beings to punish it. We surmise [that God surmised] . . . that murder might become less likely if the human blood-lust could be satisfied by meat.

". . . The specifically Jewish dietary laws are anticipated in the story of Jacob's wrestling with the mysterious being which later traditions call an angel. . . . The children of Israel *remember*, by a dietary practice [not eating the sinew of the thigh], that ambiguous and mysterious encounter. . . . They are restrained in eating, as was Jacob by the limp, but in a way that reminds of God.

"The basic anthropological sequence then as taught in Genesis, is this:

"1. A pre-human condition (garden of Eden): men eat fruit.

"2. A pre-political condition: before law . . . men eat bread, but they lapse naturally into eating meat.

"3. A political condition beginning with elementary justice and continuing to the formation of separate people (descendants of Noah after Babel): men eat meat but under law respecting blood as life. . . .

"4. A more than political condition, in which one people is brought beyond the just into some relation with the holy, eventually to aspire to holiness itself. In this condition there are further restrictions. . . .

"Why *these* dietary laws? . . . The context in which the dietary laws of Leviticus are given demonstrate that their concern is, indeed with purity and holiness. Chapter 11 is, in fact, only the first of several chapters that articulate the distinction between the clean and the unclean, the holy and the common. Each deals with what might be described as 'transgressions' of the natural boundaries, between human being and his surroundings. Chapter 11 . . . [deals with] food . . . coming from the outside in. Chapter 12 . . . [deals with] childbirth and Chapter 15, bodily issues . . . going from the inside out, and in the first and very special case, with bodily separation of one life coming out of another. Chapters 13 and 14 deal with a disease . . . of the living boundary itself, one which effaces the surfaces separating the inside from the outside which erodes and alters the human form.

". . . The principle for separating the clean from the unclean is none other than separation itself. The principles important in Genesis I—place, form or kind, motion, and life—are all at work in Leviticus 11. . . . [T]he criteria used to identify the clean and the unclean refer to their *form*, their *means of motion* and . . . what they eat to live—specifically whether they eat other animals or not. Ruled out are creatures that violate any of the principles of creation: place, form, motion and especially the original dietary code. . . . Ruled out are:

"1. Creatures that have no proper or unambiguous place, e.g. the amphibians.

"2. Creatures that have no form, especially the watery ones, (a) by virtue of having *indefinite* form with fluid shapes, lacking a firm boundary defined, say by scales—i.e. jellyfish or oysters; (b) Having *deceptive* forms like eels (fish that don't look like fish); or (c) having *incomplete* form—like the incompletely cloven-footed animals.

"3. Creatures that violate proper locomotion such as those animals that live in the water but walk on land (lobsters), those that live on land but swarm as in water (. . . in Genesis I the swarmers belonged in the water), those insects that have wings for flying but nevertheless go on all fours[,] . . . those with too many legs (centipedes) or no legs at all (that go on their belly, e.g. snakes, worms) and those who go . . . on their paws (and thus use their hands as feet).

"4. Creatures that violate the original dietary code, showing no respect for life—that is, the carnivores. . . .

"The pig is a would-be ruminant gone bad: one should chew not life but chew i.e., that which is fit for chewing. The chew-chewers are poles apart from the first accursed and most unclean animal, the belly-crawling serpent, which is, in fact, a moving digestive tract and which voraciously swallows its prey whole and alive.

"By attending to these natural differences of animal form, the dietary laws of Leviticus refine and improve upon Noachic law. . . . [T]he common principle of vitality—blood— . . . ignores and homogenizes the distinction among the kinds of animals. It shows respect for life, but not for separate living forms. Focusing only on blood ignores especially the distinction between those animals that do and those that do not honor in their eating the original separations of the world. . . .

". . . How does the making and observing of separations between the clean and the unclean conduce to holiness? What does it mean, 'Be ye holy, for I am holy?' I do not know. But I offer one observation and two suggestions.

"The dietary laws remind us not only of the created order but the order as created, not only of the intelligible separations and forms but of the mysterious source of form, separation and intelligibility. The practice of dietary laws reflects and achieves separation of the people, around the rule of separation, to celebrate through obedience the holiness and separateness of the source of separation itself—and, by the way, the bounty of food.

"And how might one become holier through observing these separations. . . . On the one hand, through obedience: one reduces the distance between the holy and the profane by sanctifying the latter through obedience to the former. The low is made high—or at least higher—through acknowledgement of its dependence on the high, the high is "brought down" . . . and given concrete expression in the forms that govern the ordinary daily life. The humdrum of existence and the passage of time are sanctified when the hallowed separateness of the Seventh Day is brought into human life and commemorated as the Sabbath. Likewise, the commonness of eating is sanctified through observance of divine commandments whose main principle reminds the mindful eaters of the supreme rule of the Holy One.

"On the other hand through imitation: God seems to say to the creature made in His image, 'You should make distinctions because I make distinctions. Because I made the separations that created the world, because I also separated you from the peoples that know Me not that you should be Mine in holiness, so you must make and honor those separations in pursuit of holiness, or more perfect godlikeness.' This suggests that it is also in the fullest rational activity that man imitates and comes closer to God—but with these important qualifications:

"We can discern distinctions in things, but we have not made them separate. Neither have we made the power of mind which registers the articulations of the world and permits us to recognize distinctions. The rational man is, therefore, only an image—and knows it. Brought by his mindful appreciation of forms before the mystery of form and mind, he must bow his head—as he alone can—to powers greater than human reason. The upright animal, his gaze uplifted and his heart filled with wonder and awe, in fact stands tallest when he freely bows his head. In order that we do not forget these qualifications, the biblical dietary laws, like the creation they memorialize and like the world we inhabit, will never be transparent to reason" (Leon Kass).[1]

THE ROAD TO THE SACRED

"The road to the sacred leads through the secular. The spirit of God rest upon the carnal, like 'the spirit that hovers over the face of the waters.' Jewish living means living according to a system of checks and balances.

"Holiness does not signify an air that prevails in the solemn atmosphere of a sanctuary, a quality reserved for supreme acts, an adverb of the spiritual, the distinction of hermits and priests. In his Great Code, Maimonides, unlike the editor of the Mishna, named the section dealing with the laws of the Temple-cult The Book of Service, while the section dealing with the laws of chastity and diet he named The Book of Holiness. The strength of holiness lies underground, in the somatic. It is primarily in the way in which we gratify physical needs that the seed of holiness is planted. Originally the holy (*kadosh*) meant that which was separated, isolated and segregated. In Jewish piety it assumed a new meaning, denoting a quality that is involved, immersed in common and earthly endeavors; carried primarily by individual, private simple deeds rather than public ceremonies. 'Man should always regard himself as if the Holy dwelled within his body, for it is written: "The Holy One is within you" (Hosea 11:9), therefore one should not mortify his body' (Taanit 11b).

"Man is the source and initiator of holiness in this world. 'If a man will sanctify himself a little, God will sanctify him more and more, if he sancti-

fies himself below, he will be sanctified from above'
(*Yoma* 39a).

"Judaism teaches us how even the gratification
of animal needs can be an act of sanctification. The
enjoyment of food may be a way of purification.
Something in my soul may be drowned in a glass
of water, when the content is gulped down as if
nothing in the world mattered except my thirst. But
we come a bit closer to God, when remembering
Him still more in excitement and passion.

"Sanctification is not an unearthly concept.
There is no dualism of the earthly and the sublime.
All things are sublime. They are all created by God
and their continuous being, their blind adherence
to the laws of necessity are, as noted above, a way
of obedience to the Creator. The existence of things
throughout the universe is a supreme ritual" (Abraham Joshua Heschel).[2]

BLESSING THE ORDINARY

"The observant Jew (the word 'observant' is correct)
. . . [blesses] the moments of the world at least one
hundred times a day. Ordinariness crowds the day,
we swim in the sense of our dailiness; and yet there
is a blessing for every separate experience of the
Ordinary.

"Jewish life is crammed with such blessings—
blessings that take note of every sight, sound, and

smell, every rising up and lying down, every mor-
sel brought to the mouth, every act of cleansing. . . .
When he breaks his bread, he will bless God for
having 'brought forth bread from the earth.' Each
kind of food is similarly blessed in turn. . . . And
when the meal is done, a thanksgiving is said
for the whole of it, and table-songs are sung with
exultation.

"'The world and its provisions, in short, are
observed —in the two meanings of 'observe.' Creation is both noticed and felt to be sanctified.
Everything is minutely paid attention to, and then
ceremoniously praised. . . . But these celebrations
through noticing are not self-centered and do not
stop at humanity. . . . There is a blessing on wit
nessing lightning, falling stars, great mountains
and deserts. . . . From the stone to the human
being, creatureliness is extolled.

"The huge and unending shower of blessings
. . . serves us doubly: in the first place, what you
are taught to praise you will not maim or exploit
or destroy. In the second place, the categories and
impulses of Art become the property of the simplest
soul: because it is all the handiwork of the Creator,
everything Ordinary is seen as Extraordinary. The
world, and every moment in it, is seen to be sublime, and not merely *seen to be*, but brought home
to the intensest part of consciousness. . . .

"The Jew has this in common with the artist:
he means nothing to be lost on him[;] . . . nothing
that passes before him is taken for granted, everything is exalted. If we are enjoined to live in the
condition of noticing all things—or, to put it more

extremely but more exactly, in the condition of awe, *how can we keep ourselves from sliding off from awe of God's creation to worship of God's creation*? And does it matter if we do?

"The difference, the reason it matters, is a single and shattering one: the difference is what keeps us from being idolaters.

"What is an idol? Anything that is allowed to come between ourselves and God. Anything that is *instead of* God. . . . The Creator is not contained within his own Creation; the Creator is incarnate in nothing, and is free of any image or imagining. God is not any part of Nature; or in any part of Nature; God is not any man, or in any man. When we praise nature or man or any experience or work of man, we are worshipping the Creator and the Creator alone. . . .

"It is not true, as we so often hear, that Judaism is a developmental religion, that there is a progression upward from Moses to the Prophets. The Prophets enjoined backsliders to renew themselves through the Mosaic idea, . . . [that] has survived unmodified, 'Take heed of yourselves, that your heart be not deceived and ye turn aside, and serve some other gods and worship them' (Deuteronomy 11:16). This perception has never been superseded. To seem to supersede it is to transgress it. . . .

"There is no Instead Of. There is only the creator. God is alone. That is what we mean when we utter the ultimate idea which is the pinnacle of the Mosaic revolution in human perception: God is one. . . .

"The child of a friend of mine was taken to the Egyptian galleries of the museum. In a glass case stood the figure of a cat resplendent in the perfection of its artfulness—long-necked, gracile, cryptic, authoritative, beautiful, spiritual. 'I understand,' said the child, 'how they wanted to bow down to the cat, I feel the same.' And then she said a Hebrew word:—*asur*—forbidden—the great hallowed No which tumbles down the centuries from Sinai, the No that can rise up only out of the abundant celebrations and blessings of Yes, Yes, Yes, the shower of Yeses that praise fragrant oils, and wine, and sex, and scholars, and thunder, and new clothes and falling stars, and washing your hands before eating" (Cynthia Ozick).[3]

NOTES

1. Kass, excerpts from "Why the Dietary Laws?", pp. 42–48.

2. Heschel, *Man is Not Alone*, pp. 265–267.

3. Cynthia Ozick, "The Riddle of the Ordinary," in *Art & Ardor: Essays* (New York: Alfred A. Knopf Inc., 1983), pp. 204–209.

Bibliography

BOOKS

Adler, Mortimer, ed. *Encyclopaedia Britannica, Micro-padeaia.* 15th ed. Chicago: 1992.

Agnon, Shmuel Yosef. *Days of Awe.* New York: Schocken Books, 1965.

Biale, David. *Eros and the Jews.* New York: Basic Books, 1992.

Bokser, Ben-Zion, ed. *Rabbi Abraham Isaac Kook.* Trans. Ben-Zion Bokser. Mahwah, NJ: Paulist Press, 1978.

Chill, Abraham. *The Mitzvoth—The Commandments and Their Rationale.* Jerusalem: Keter, 1972.

Dresner, Samuel, Siegel, Seymour, and Pollack, David. *The Jewish Dietary Laws.* Revised and expanded edition. New York: Rabbinical Assembly of America and the United Commission on Jewish Education, 1982.

Friedman, Thomas. *From Beirut to Jerusalem.* New York: Farrar, Strauss, Giroux, 1989.

Gerber, Jane S. *The Jews of Spain*. New York: Free
   Press, 1994.
ha-Levi, Aaron. *Sefer haHinnuch*. Trans. Charles Wen-
   grow. Jerusalem and New York: Feldheim Publish-
   ers, 1978.
Hartman, David. *A Living Covenant: The Innovative
   Spirit in Traditional Judaism*. Glencoe, IL.: The Free
   Press, 1985.
Hertz, J. H., ed. *The Pentateuch and the Haftorahs*. N.p.:
   Metzudah, 1937.
Heschel, Abraham Joshua. "A Pattern for Living." In
   Man is Not Alone. New York: Noonday Press, 1994.
Hirsch, Samson Raphael. *The Pentateuch*. Gateshead,
   England: Judaica Press Ltd., 1982.
Hochstein, Peter. *Up from Seltzer—A Handy Guide to
   4 Jewish Generations*. New York: Workman Pub-
   lishing, 1981.
Kaplan, Mordecai. *Judaism as a Civilization*. New York:
   Schocken Books, 1967.
Kasher, Menahem. *Encyclopedia of Biblical Interpreta-
   tions—A Millennial Anthology*. Volume 2: Genesis.
   Trans. Harry Freedman. New York: American Bib-
   lical Encyclopedia Society, 1955.
Kushner, Harold. *To Life*. Boston: Little Brown, 1993.
Leibowitz, Nehama. *Studies in Leviticus*. Jerusalem:
   World Zionist Organization, 1980.
Lubavitch Women's Organization. *Body and Soul—
   A Handbook for Kosher Living*. Brooklyn, NY:
   Lubavitch Women's Cookbook Publications, 1989.
Maimonides. *The Guide of the Perplexed*. Trans.
   Shlomo Pines. Chicago: University of Chicago Press,
   1963.
Munk, Elie. *The Call of the Torah—Genesis*. Trans.
   E. Z. Mazer. Jerusalem: Feldheim Publishers, 1980.

————— *The Call of the Torah—Vayikra*. Trans. E. Z. Mazer. Brooklyn, NY: ArtScroll Mesorah Series, 1992.

Neusner, Jacob. *The Midrash: An Introduction*. Northvale, NJ: Jason Aronson Inc., 1990.

Newman, Louis. *The Hasidic Anthology*. New York: Schocken Paperbacks, 1968.

Orlinsky, Harry, ed. *The Torah—The Five Books of Moses*. Philadelphia: Jewish Publication Society of America, 1962.

Ozick, Cynthia. "The Riddle of the Ordinary." In *Art and Ardor: Essays*. New York: Alfred A. Knopf Inc., 1983.

Petuchowski, Jakob. *Heirs of the Pharisees*. Brown Classics in Judaica. Lanham, MD: University Press of America, 1986.

Philo of Alexandria. *The Works of Philo*. Trans. C. D. Yonge. Vinton, VA: Hendrickson, 1993.

Plaut, Gunther, ed. *The Torah—A Modern Commentary*. New York: Union of American Hebrew Congregations, 1983.

Ramban. *Commentary of the Torah—Leviticus*. Trans. Charles Chavel. New York: Shiloh, 1974.

Rosenbloom, Noah. *Tradition in an Age of Reform— The Religious Philosophy of Samson Raphael Hirsch*. Philadelphia: Jewish Publication Society of America, 1976.

Rosenbloom, Noah. *Luzzato's Ethico-Psychological Interpretation of Judaism*. New York: Yeshiva University Press, 1965.

Roth, Cecil, ed. *Encyclopaedia Judaica*. Jerusalem: Keter, 1972.

Saperstein, Marc, ed. *Jewish Preaching 1200–1800: An Anthology*. New Haven, CT: Yale University Press, 1989.

Scherman, Nosson, and Zlotowitz, Meir, eds. *The ArtScroll Weekday Siddur*. Trans. Nosson Scherman. Brooklyn, NY: Mesorah Publications, 1988.

Scholem, Gershom. *Major Trends in Jewish Mysticism*. New York: Schocken Paperbacks, 1961.

Schwartz, Leo. *Wolfson of Harvard—Portrait of a Scholar*. Philadelphia: Jewish Publication Society of America, 1978.

Schwartz, Richard. *Introduction to Judaism and Vegetarianism*. 2d ed. Marblehead, MA: Micah Publications, 1988.

Sheinkopf, David. *Gelatin in Jewish Law*. New York: Bloch Press, 1982.

Steinsaltz, Adin, *The Strife of the Spirit*. Northvale, NJ: Jason Aronson Inc., 1988.

U. S. Bureau of Census. *Statistical Abstract of the United States: 1993*. 113th. ed. Washington, D.C: U. S. GPO, 1993.

❦

JOURNALS, MAGAZINES, AND NEWSPAPERS

Alter, Robert. "A New Theory of Kashrut." *Commentary*, August 1979.

Anderson, John Ward. "Poachers Felling World's Tigers, Rhinos." *Washington Post*, November 29, 1994.

Avery, Dennis. "Don't Worry, Eat and Be Happy." *Wall Street Journal*, December 11, 1995.

Bennetts, Leslie. "k.d. lang Cuts It Close." *Vanity Fair*, August 1993.

Chafetz, Ze'ev. "A Wedding in Exile." *Jerusalem Report*, October 24, 1994.

Cohn, D'Vera. "Local Fish Still Pose Health Risk." *Washington Post*, December 1, 1994.

Fall, Albert. "Seeking Ways of Making Food Acceptable to Jews and Moslems." *Cornell Chronicle*, October 1, 1992.

Florman, Judy. "Kosher Dining in Los Angeles." *Kashrus Magazine—The Magazine for the Kosher Consumer* (Brooklyn, NY), February 1995.

Ginsberg, Allen. "C'mon Pigs of Western Civilization Eat More Grease." *City Lights Review*, August 1994.

Haffkine, W. M. "A Plea for Orthodoxy." *Menorah Journal*, April 18, 1916.

Hwang, Suein. "Kosher Food Firms Dive into the Mainstream." *Wall Street Journal*, April 1, 1993.

Kass, Leon. "Why the Dietary Laws?" *Commentary*, June 1994.

Lubavitcher Rebbe. "The Common Denominator." *L'Chayim Newsletter for All Jews*, issue 230, September 12, 1992.

Marantz, Felice. "My Dinner with Mimi." *Jerusalem Report*, December 29, 1994.

Mogelonsky, Marcia. "Kiss Me You Kosher Fool." *American Demographics*, May 1994.

Moore, Stephen. "So Much for Scarce Resources." *Public Interest*, Winter 1994.

Prager, Dennis. "Should a Modern Jew Keep Kosher?" *Brandeis-Bardin Institute Newsletter*, Spring 1980, November–December 1980.

Rosen, David. "Survey Links Day School Experience with Jewish Identity." *Yeshiva University Review*, Winter 1995.

Press, Newtol. "Kosher Ecology." *Commentary*, February 1985.

Regenstein, Joe, and Regenstein, Carol. "Looking In."

Kashrus Magazine—The Magazine for the Kosher Consumer (Brooklyn, NY), February 1995.

Shapiro, Haim. "Kippot Scarce at Opening of World's First Kosher McDonald's." *Jerusalem Post,* October 12, 1995.

Shields, Mark. "Return of the Pander Bear." *Washington Post,* January 19, 1995.

Silverman, Edward. "Kosher Hot Dog Industry Is Losing Family Flavor." *Forward,* September 1, 1995.

Sugarman, Carole, and Evans, Sandra. "'Low Fat': Heavy on Promises, Light on proof." *Washington Post,* March 15, 1995.

"Symposium of Kosher Law and Modern Technology." *Kashrus Magazine—The Magazine for the Kosher Consumer* (Brooklyn, NY), February 1995.

INTERNET

"Frequently Asked Questions on Soc.Culture.Jewish." *America Online,* January 31, 1995, Part 4 (Observance), Subject 6.9.

"Frequently asked Questions on Soc.Culture.Jewish." *PSINET,* January 4, 1995, Part 7 (Jews as a Nation), Subject 13.5.

John Davis, British Vegetarian Society, "Information Sheets" John@portsveg.demon.co.UK.

Credits

The author gratefully acknowledges permission to quote from the following sources:

newed © 1979 by Sylvia Heschel. Reprinted by permission of Farrar, Straus & Giroux, Inc.

From "Am I Feeding an Army . . . or Nurturing a Nation" by Tziporah Muchnik in *Body and Soul*. Copyright © 1989 by Lubavitch Women's Cookbook Publications. Reprinted by permission of the publisher.

From *Days of Awe* by Shmuel Joseph Agnon. Copyright © 1965 by Schocken Books. Reprinted by permission of Pantheon Books, Inc., a division of Random House.

From *From Beirut to Jerusalem* by Thomas Friedman. Copyright © 1989 by Farrar, Straus & Giroux. Reprinted by permission of Farrar, Straus & Giroux, Inc.

From *Heirs of the Pharisees* by Jakob Petuchowski. Copyright © 1986 by Brown Classics in Judaica. Reprinted by permission of Jacob Neusner, editor of the Brown Classics in Judaica.

From *Judaism as a Civilization* by Mordecai Kaplan. Copyright © 1967 by Schocken Books. Reprinted by permission of Schocken Books, published by Pantheon Books, a division of Random House.

From "Kosher Ecology" by Newtol Press. Copyright © 1985 by *Commentary*. Reprinted from COMMENTARY, February 1985, by permission; all rights reserved.

From "Kosher Living, Healthy Living" by Kenneth Storch in *Body and Soul*. Copyright © 1989 by Lubavitch Women's Cookbook Publications. Reprinted by permission of the publisher.

From preface to *Judaism and Vegetarianism* by Richard H. Schwartz. Copyright © 1988 by Richard H. Schwartz. Published by Micah Publications. Reprinted by permission of Richard H. Schwartz.

From *Major Trends in Jewish Mysticism* by Gerson Scholem. Copyright © 1941 by Schocken Publishing House, Jerusalem. Reprinted by permission of Schocken Books. Published by Pantheon Books, a division of Random House, Inc.

From "My Dinner with Mimi" by Felice Marantz. Copyright © 1994 by *The Jerusalem Report*. Reprinted from *The Jerusalem Report*, December 29, 1994, by permission of Jerusalem Report Publications.

From ABRAHAM ISAAC KOOK, translated by Ben Zion Bokser. Copyright © 1978 by Ben Zion Bokser. Used by permission of Paulist Press.

From "Should a Modern Jew Keep Kosher?" by Dennis Prager in *Brandeis-Bardin Institute Newsletter*, Spring 1980 and November–December, 1980. Copyright © 1980 by Dennis Prager. Reprinted by permission of Dennis Prager.

From *Studies in Leviticus* by Nehama Leibowitz. Copyright © 1980 by World Zionist Organization. Reprinted by permission of The Department for Torah Education and Culture in the Diaspora, Joint Authority for Jewish Zionist Education.

From "Symposium of Kosher Law and Modern Technology," *Kashrus Magazine—The Magazine for the Kosher Consumer* (Brooklyn, NY),

Index

ABOUT THE AUTHOR

Irving Welfeld is a senior analyst in the Department of Housing and Urban Development and was formerly an attorney in the department's Office of General Counsel. The author is a graduate of Yeshiva Torah Vodaath, Yeshiva University High School for Boys, Brooklyn College, and Harvard Law School. Mr. Welfeld has been admitted to the bar in New York, Massachusetts, and the District of Columbia. He has served as the Robert LaFollete Visiting Distinguished Professor at the University of Wisconsin in Madison and as a consultant to the U.S. Civil Rights Commission. He is the author of articles that have appeared in law and housing journals and the *Public Interest*. He has also written two books, *Where We Live* and *HUD Scandals—Howling Headlines and Silent Fiascoes*. He and his wife, Harriet, live in Rockville, Maryland.